BEST
PUB WALKS
IN ESSEX

Derek Keeble

Published by Sigma Leisure – an imprint of
Sigma Press, 1 South Oak Lane, Wilmslow, Cheshire SK9 6AR, England.

British Library Cataloguing in Publication Data
A CIP record for this book is available from the British Library.

ISBN: 1-85058-380-3

Typesetting and Design by: Sigma Press, Wilmslow, Cheshire.

Cover: Photograph by Roy Tover

Printed by: Manchester Free Press

Preface

Thank you for looking closer at this book. Perhaps the book was gift-wrapped for you, or maybe you will purchase a copy if you have not already done so. It is a book about walking in the splendid countryside of Essex, where walkers rely upon inns and public houses for sustenance whilst away from home. The 31 walks have been selected to give a range of walking environments in the county of Essex.

Background: Estimates account for fifteen hundred pubs scattered over the county, and for several thousand miles of pedestrian rights-of-way veined around them. The author has not sampled beer at all the pubs, but he has visited a great many of them in the course of walking (and jogging) on a majority of the footways in each of the fourteen districts of Essex.

Walks: The thirty-one circular rambles are in countryside suitable for a real treat – a walk which can be completed between meals. They are among the better ones of their kind in Essex, and very probably the best. In each case the pub is used as a base for the walk where a car-park is available for patrons, once given the landlord's permission to do so. In many cases, public transport is available.

Views: The walks seek to give a blend of countryside textures, with arresting long and short-range views, the beauties of which are for the beholder to perceive. Attention is given to the contour detail so that the horizon varies in an attractive way.

The County: Essex is one of the Home Counties, situated on the coastal side of London, covering more than three thousand square kilometres north of the River Thames. It is a heavily populated county with a vast arable landscape peppered with jewels such as finely restored manor houses, exquisite village churches and accommodating pubs. The predominant surface is clay, either boulder or Eocene, both of which are slippery when wet, despite having adhesive qualities.

Footwear with a tread pattern which will combat wet clay is advised. As well as Thames-speak; you will hear the rural Essex accent – "Oi hev wun". Some vowels have a touch of 'strine, but the speech is rooted in East Anglia, just as East Saxons were involved with the Anglo-Saxon times.

Essex brewery: Beer is the traditional thirst-quencher. How often has a rambler's pace imperceptibly increased when the roof of a pub peeps over the horizon? 1993 saw the Essex Brewers Ridleys enjoying the accolade of Britain's best bitter brewers of the previous year. Ridleys of Essex were succeeded by Adnams of Suffolk with a similar award. That makes quaffing a local pint even more enjoyable.

Pubs: Britain deserves its reputation for being a nation of inventive people. One of the best inventions was the British pub. Abused by some? Perhaps. Strangled by some regulations? Maybe: yet they still connive to get the brewers' best products to the lips of the thirsty in convivial circumstances. A phone call will ascertain what food is available and when. There are only two sorts of pubs considered. Those which are welcoming, comfortable and open to serve, and those which are closed or fail to welcome strangers. Alas, only 31 examples of the first category can be included here. None of the second sort are. Salutations go to all those landlords and ladies patiently waiting to serve us.

Pub Yarns The final paragraphs for each walk offer some information about the area walked. They separate notes of interest from walk directions, because it is irksome to scan through anecdotal verbiage when looking for a specific field directional clue. A Yarn could just be the topic of conversation which may lead to one of those ephemeral friendships which are part of the warmth of British pubs.

Landowners: Both landlords and landowners feature in a book about walking in the countryside. Public rights-of-way are invariably on somebody else's property. The public has a right to use them, but does not own them. There are highway laws which govern the use and maintenance of these pedestrian ways. Some landowners find the laws too irksome to obey and are not familiar with The Rights of Way Act 1990. Luckily more show a pride in their land management of our inheritance and reveal a respect of the law of the land. To them, the goodwill of the walking public – a large part of their market – is more important than subsidised profit from field-path crops. Our thanks to them too.

Law of The Land Laws, such as the The Rights of Way Act 1990, need authority to uphold them, and in the case of highways, local authorities shoulder the burden. Many local government officers have worked to assist volunteers in the upkeep of the field-path network, and they too receive our gratitude.

District Councils: are mentioned in *walk details*, but the chief authority is the County Council's Highways Engineer at County Hall, Chelmsford. Field edge paths should be a walkable 1.5m (nearly six feet) in width, and crossfield paths 1m wide, clear of overhanging crops.

The Walks: Descriptions are allied to the 'Roy Tover' schematic maps to give a field-by-field account of progress. The 16 cardinal points are abbreviated SSE etc. and linear features in the countryside, mostly man-made, act as handrails. This works well, but sometimes relocation is necessary, and for this reason map references are given to unite the walk to details on a Pathfinder Map.

Sketch Maps: The schematic maps are designed to complement the Ordnance Survey sheets. An explanation of the use of map references, of handrails, of the author's pacing standard, and of a simple compass technique are all included.

Getting to the Walks: In each case notes indicate an approach by road from one of the major roads through Essex: the M25 London orbital motorway; the M11 London to Cambridge; the A12 trunk road, London to Great Yarmouth; and the A604 road Market Harborough to Harwich. Trains and buses are not forgotten, and where appropriate, information about these connections are given. Pubs, buses and trains are currently in a state of flux, and up-to-date timetabling should be consulted to reinforce the information given in this book.

Walks Survey The field findings for all 31 Walks in this book were made between January 1st and June 30th 1993. The first walk was "The favourite walk" until the second walk revised opinion, and so on. Finally there were just thirty-one favourite walks. The intention is for you to have an opportunity to enjoy them too. Essex is a grand county to explore on foot.

The Map Reader's Toolkit is a glimpse into a map-reading art. For example it shows how a compass can convert NNE from the book to an actual direction in the field, and how to locate a six-figure reference on a map. By the means outlined, all thirty-one walks were completed without mishap, and it is hoped the enjoyment can be repeated by you.

Whether you use this book alone in an armchair or out with friends on the fieldpaths of Essex, best wishes for happy feet and refreshing drinks.

Derek Keeble

CONTENTS

MEANDERINGS THROUGH VERDANT VALLEYS

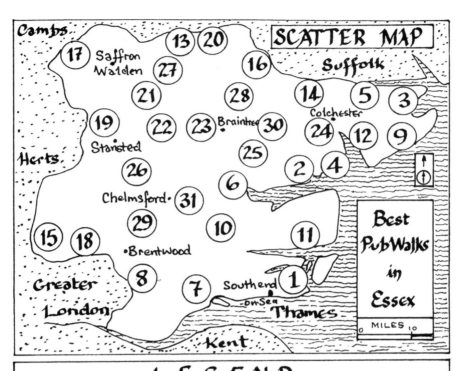

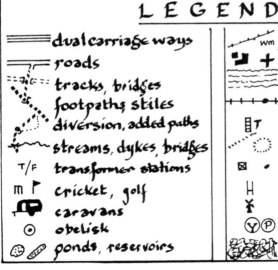

dual carriage ways

roads

tracks, bridges

footpaths, stiles

diversion, added paths

streams, dykes, bridges

T/F transformer stations

m cricket, golf

caravans

obelisk

ponds, reservoirs

wm boundaries, waymarks

buildings, churches

sea

railway, station

T steps, telephone

embankments

pylons, poles

H recreation grounds

windmills

YP relocation check, park

woodland

1

GO WALKING IN ESSEX!

Walking is a great exercise which does not strain resources of time and money. It is a simple habit to start, and it makes a nice hobby which often opens avenues to new interests. It is a form of exercise which most people find they are able to maintain.

Fitness means different things to different people. Many people measure fitness by their speed of recovery to normal pulse after a little brisk walking (3 minutes per 200 metres, no faster to begin with). Walking, they say, can help relieve tension and stress.

WALK WHERE?

Pamphlet   Public access in the countryside is summarised in a free booklet *Out In The Country* from The Countryside Commission Publications CCP232, Printworks Lane, Levenshulme, Manchester, M19 3JP.

Charter   Public footpaths should be visible and in walkable condition. On such paths it is easy to follow a dictum of the *Countryside Access Charter* "Keep to public paths across farmland". Sometimes permissive paths are made available but they can be revoked at any time. Only Public Footpaths endure as highways of the realm.

Parkland   Other places such as public parks and open spaces also make good walks, as Walk 15 in this book demonstrates.

What Equipment?

Every rambier has her or his own idea of the best equipment. The single outfit suitable for all occasions has yet to be designed. A choice of equipment is needed.

Footwear The best footwear is made by Smith & Nephew Plc. It is thin medical tacky tape. For first aid it should be applied to any part of the foot susceptible to blisters. To apply it over a blister is second aid. Boots, shoes, trainers, wellies are all suitable, one pair at a time, provided they have the potential to be comfortable for two hours, and they have a tread pattern likely to counter sticky, slippery Essex clay. Plastic over-bags for muddy boots in pubs are courteous and considerate.

Legs Leggings or over-trousers? Watch golfers on a wet day and follow the example you like best. A round of golf can take around two hours, just like a walk from this book.

Body The torso likes layers. A wicking layer next to the skin and then a shirt or blouse, followed by two thin woollies and not one thick one. As cricketers robe and disrobe their sweaters, so walkers can add or subtract to the number of warmth retainers at any time. Top this off with a weather-proof cagoule.

Head And Hands Hat and gloves worn according to need.

Accoutrements A small bag like a school **rucksack** in which to carry those discarded jumpers. Spare umpires are seldom found in the countryside. An **umbrella** is a useful tool, except on windy days. It keeps off the rain without overheating the walker. It is also useful as a flag to warn motorists that pedestrians are bravely facing the oncoming traffic. Relevant **maps**, and a **compass**. When a map is dropped, it shows displeasure by gliding as a seaplane to the nearest large puddle. A clear plastic bag used as a map case frustrates it.

Pedometer or **Opisometer** or both. The latter is a better tool.

Ultra-sonic wave emitters, as used by postal workers, are good for warding off unwanted attention from dogs, cattle and horses.

A **walking stick** is more than an emblem for the elderly. It can plumb depths, feel for bridges, knock back brambles, ward off animals, pull companions out of ditches, point out distant objects of interest, and scratch messages in the mud. Many motorists give pedestrians with a walking stick more passing space.

WALK WHEN?

Don't wait for a holiday. Start preparing for one now. Early morning walks are good, as are summer evening and weekend rambles. Rambles are organised every day of the year somewhere in Essex. Busy gardening times like September and March are also the best walking times. The better walking season in the fertile lowlands is August to April. Arable crops then deny the use of some paths until the harvest in early August. Eccentric night walking, other than sleep walking, does happen.

HOW TO WALK?

Etiquette   Everybody knows how to walk, but not so many are sure about established walking etiquette. Public paths are on other people's property; one walks respectfully and certainly not disrespectfully.

Paths   Paths may be left in a state disrespectful of your intended usage; e.g. having crops, other than grass, which prevent the line of the path being apparent on the ground. In these cases, the procedure is make the best of them for the time being, and then to report the matter to the highway authority soon afterwards. Councils do not have an army of engineers inspecting the paths; except the fragmented army with which you march. Your reports are important to the walkers following in the next decade.

Clubs   If you join or form a walking group, take your turn at leading a walk, or if you cannot do this, fulfil some other helpful role.

Pubs   Treat pubs respectfully too. If you have a flask in the
                         rucksack for emergencies, leave it there, do not
                         broach it on pub premises. Even if your boots look
                         clean, they may be muddy underneath. Change shoes,
                         or pull on bags before going indoors.

ALL THIS WITH WHOM?

Groups   Family groups, friendship fours or meets of people
                         from other hobbies are often seen walking. It is better
                         to be with somebody; or if alone, ensure somebody
                         knows your expected time of return from an intended
                         route.

National associations like the Youth Hostels Association, The Ramblers'
Association and The Long Distance Walkers' Association each have a
network of local groups.

Parish councils, urban wards and neighbourhood watch communities
often have walking meets for social contacts.

Holidays   Holiday walking organisations have local follow-up
                         groups where people can keep fit until the next
                         holiday.

What's On   Look and listen around for *What's On* in newspapers,
                         local radio and libraries. Try one. Most organisations
                         expect enquirers. If you do not like that group, try
                         another, and when you are sure, join. The cost is not
                         once-off, like a marriage licence fee. Rambling clubs
                         usually operate an annual fee system for which you
                         get a sort of local walking calendar.

Directories   Both Essex and Suffolk County Councils produce
                         directories of walk publications, and most outdoor
                         organisations have someone who knows of a
                         threshold to the walking experience.

Keep fit with happy feet!

2

Walking Hints & Tips

The basic information about pedestrian highways is best relayed by maps. Maps produced by The Ordnance Survey for publication by Her Majesty's Stationery Office are very good at showing highway lines clearly. Three scales of map come in to the walker's range.

1. DEFINITIVE MAPS

These are OS sheets at 1:10,000 scale upon which the highway authority (in Essex 1993 it is Essex County Council) has recorded the lawful existence of a highway. They are expensive to buy, even as base sheets, and they are not suitable for use in the field. A map big enough to cover the terrain needed for a two-hour walk, would be so large it would sail-off and give the map-reader a hang-gliding experience. They are best kept in the cabinets of local government offices where they may be consulted during reasonable office hours.

2. LANDRANGER MAPS

These are very good value for armchair planning, and for finding the way to the rendezvous. Scaled at 1:50,000 they do not give much information about the fields through which the red dot symbols for footpaths run. In an area of good path husbandry, where the paths are in a lawful state, then the Landranger is perfectly adequate for local fieldpath walking.

3. PATHFINDER MAPS

These are the old two-and-a-half inch series of maps in smart new format. These 1:25,000 sheets are the ideal tool for the explorer of paths in the countryside. They carry sufficient information to allow smart re-locations to take place when things are not going so well.

All maps, including the Roy Tover schematic maps drawn in 1993, are soon out of date in part. Mankind is restless, forever changing the face of The Earth. A new fence here, an orchard gone from there, cows replaced by golfers, and like changes occur too rapidly for the cartographer to draw. The map-reader has to allow for this when out in the field.

Map References

Six-figure map references are used liberally to help reconcile the Roy Tover map with the Pathfinder sheet and with the terrain. It is a well-tried system giving a location to the nearest 99 metres. Here is a rehearsal of the skill.

1. Observe the map has an overprinted grid with the lines numbered around the margins. The spaces between the lines are not numbered.

2. The enumeration is left to right, as we read; and bottom to top.

3. Split the six figures in half. For example, 949875 becomes 949 and 875.

4. Insert invisible decimal points to give tens, units and tenths as 94.9 and 87.5.

5. The first set is applied to the EASTINGS and the second set to the NORTHINGS. The initial letters **E** and **N** are in alphabetical order.

6. The Eastings on the map are the left to right numbers. Move along to line 94 and nine tenths of the way across the space to 95. Now go up the Northings as far as line 87 and guesstimate five tenths over the space towards line 88. Where 94.9 and 87.5 intersect, is the location sought.

7. These numbers recur nationwide, so a prefix such as TL or TQ is used to separate them. Thus TQ949875 is on Pathfinder TQ 98, and should be near Great Wakering's Anchor.

Using Gather Features And Handrails

The most common map-reading error is to travel too far. Human beings, they say, are basically lazy, so why should they walk too far? Perhaps because it is easier to continue enjoying oneself, rather than interrupt the enjoyment with an uneasy change in trajectory. Whatever the reason, the practical remedy is to deploy a **gather feature** or two.

Gather Features

A common example of a gather feature is as a landmark used when giving directions to puzzled motorists. "Turn round, and go back as far as The Flying Fox and its the first shop beyond the pub." In such a helpful response, *The Flying Fox* is a gather feature. It alerts a change in the mode of travel. If it is missed, the motorist is even more puzzled, and he or she asks somebody else for renewed instructions.

Countryside Landmarks

Gather features in the countryside are not so pronounced as pubs. Corners of fields, pylon wires crossing the line of travel, bridges, crests of hills etc. have to act as gather features. Not all gather features are exactly at the point of action, as *The Flying Fox* was in the example given. Sometimes the feature occurs before the crucial location is reached. Conversely, the gather feature might be beyond the target, like a sort of safety net which should not be missed.

Three-minute Check

To reinforce the use of gather features, back them up by using a watch. For example, "I need to turn left after a quarter of a mile. My pace is 24 minutes for a mile. The time is now 09.50. I should find my gather feature at 09.56". Check it out, as they say.

Handrailing

The expression comes from using a handrail on a staircase or footbridge. The technique transfers to the countryside when visual, rather than touching, handrails are used to steer by. Lowland landscapes, such as Essex, are very much man-made with many linear artifacts. There are enough of them to relegate the use of a compass to a supportive role. The essential skills are in selecting the best handrail from the map and following the correct one on the terrain.

Handrails are hedges, ditches, boundaries, overhead cables, surfaced strips and so on. Natural handrails are valleys and ridges. Anything linear is a handrail.

Fragmentation

Not all handrails will begin where you begin, stay adjacent to your chosen route, and finish where you want to finish. Some will be parallel a little way off but visible; or as in the case of Walk 15, only visible for short intervals. Some will converge towards your route, some diverge away, and it may be necessary to use more than one in any three-minute period. As with using gather features, the watch is a useful tool to back up the use of handrails. It is not necessary to walk with the map continuously in focus. On the other hand, there is no point in having a map if it is not used. A check every three minutes is sufficient to keep control of the course.

Pacing

The pacing of social group walks invariably causes comment. Any leader can be accused of being both too fast and too slow simultaneously by members of the group. The problem of pleasing all of the people all of the time exists, and it will not be solved by this book.

Pace

A reasonable compromise based on the experience of leading hundreds of social group walks in and around Essex is 15 minutes per kilometre, or 4 km per hour. It is the pace adopted in this book. This compares with the 1993 United Kingdom AAA 10 kilometre walk for men which was won at about 4 minutes per kilometre, or with the 5 kilometre walk for women won at about 4.5 minutes per kilometre. Even these athletic times are adrift from the current world records, despite being more than three times faster than the 15 minutes per km of this book!

What happens if you find this book's pace is too slow for you? Suppose you find 90 minutes is sufficient to complete a suggested 120 minute walk. It is good that you know what *your* pace is. It requires a 25% reduction from any of the given duration times. Conversely, if the given pace is too fast, just add the necessary percentage to the given duration times. A bit like adjusting a pedometer, perhaps!

Time for stoppages needs to be added to the given duration times, of course.

Why Kilometres?

Ordnance Survey maps are overprinted with a grid of kilometre squares, at whatever scale, therefore, each map has a handy built-in measurer, used for guesstimates of distance. At the prescribed pace, it takes fifteen minutes to walk a kilometre.

Kilometres and miles have a common relative; the furlong. When athletics changed from imperial to metric measure, the tracks were not substantially altered. Once round the track used to be 440 yards. Now once around the same track is 400 metres. One circuit is two furlongs.

A furlong, therefore is useful for conversions from miles to kilometres and the reverse. It is also very useful when estimating distances in the field; less cumbersome than hundreds of yards or metres.

As it is also easy to divide a mapped kilometre in to five, the humble furlong comes in handy as a map-reader's tool. It is also a fifth of a square on a map. In the field it is the distance Linford Christie or John Regis and their rivals cover in about 20 seconds on a track. At country walking speed, it takes three minutes to walk a furlong (220 yards or 200 metres), unless the pub is close, when stride rhythms often increase.

Three-Minute Lapse

Check locations every three minutes. If wrong, it takes three minutes to get back to the last safe location. That is only six minutes lost (5% of two hours) and is much better than losing a whole hour.

Motorists

Road length measure in Great Britain remains unconverted, therefore miles are used in this book, because they relate more easily to the language of road signs etc.

Compass Aid with 16 Cardinals

Walking in the Essex countryside and navigating with the handrailing technique ensures simple compass skills are seldom used. Consequently there is a loss of confidence when the skill is required. Sometimes the exit on the further side of the field is temporarily out of view, and a compass bearing would help to locate it. Here is a rehearsal drill using the versatile Silva or Suunto type compass which can read angles on the map and in the terrain. Observe that there are four arrows to manipulate:

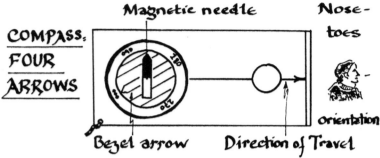

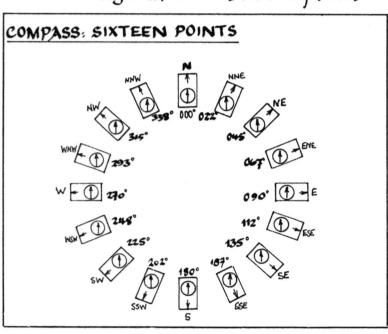

a. The direction of TRAVEL arrow along the base plate, probably going through the magnifier.

b. The rotating chamber containing the magnet has some parallel lines across it, with the centre pointed to the zero on the calibrations around the bezel. Call this the BEZEL arrow.

c. The Northern end of the magnet, frequently red or luminous, the MAGNETIC arrow or needle.

d. Your own orientation, your NOSE-TOES arrow.

Walking on a Bearing

1. Rotate the bezel so that the required bearing reads off against the direction of TRAVEL arrow.

The required bearings for the sixteen cardinal points used in this book are (in degrees):

N	000
NNE	022
NE	045
ENE	067
E	090
ESE	112
SE	135
SSE	157
S	180
SSW	202
SW	225
WSW	248
W	270
WNW	293
NW	315
NNW	338
N	360 or 000.

2. Disregard all improbabilities and imagine you are wearing a Cross-your-Heart garment. Hold the compass in front of the X, level and away from magnetic influences, such as portable phones, and with the TRAVEL arrow pointing the same way as the NOSE-TOES alignment.

3. Perform the ultimate increment of the Hokey-Cokey and turn your whole self around, until such time as the MAGNETIC needle is pointing the same way as the BEZEL arrow.

4. With BEZEL and MAGNETIC co-incident, and TRAVEL and NOSE-TOES co-incident, look up to AIM at a landmark and walk in that direction. Repeat the process if necessary.

Taking a Bearing off the Map

How do I know the bearing I want if I prefer not to use SSE, NW and all that jargon? Easier still! Forget the MAGNETIC needle and the NOSE-TOES arrow. Just place the base plate on the map so the TRAVEL arrow is aligned from where you ARE towards where you want to BE. Hold map and compass steady in that position as you rotate the chamber until the BEZEL arrow is aligned with the North (towards top of mapped words) GRID lines on the map.

5. Take compass off map. Look at the bezel reading by the TRAVEL arrow line; that is the required bearing from Grid North.

Eight Estimates

Walking in the countryside, reading a map as you go, is also an exercise in calculation. An estimate has always to be balanced against new clues. Mild problems pour in, and their successful resolution gives another facet to the satisfaction of country walking as a physical and recreational exercise. The eight essential estimates are really four in number. They occur twice, once on the map and again in the terrain, to total eight.

Direction

Bearings are measured from North. Britain uses degrees up to 360. The four cardinal points, north, east, south and west can be divided and sub-divided to give sixteen, as used in this book. Official documents often use such directional pointers.

Magnetic Variation

The zero of grid north on the map is slightly different from the magnetic zero registered with a compass needle. Mariners allow for this variation, but the difference between magnetic north of the compass, and grid north of the map, is so slender a wedge, that no field in Essex is wide enough to warrant calculation of it.

Further, a hand-held compass will deflect with the acts of breathing and walking, to give more deviation than magnetic variation. Therefore ignore calculating Variation, until you need to cross some featureless tract.

1. On a map, north is indicated by grid lines, by the orientation of major printing, with ascending strokes poking northwards, and by notes in the legend.

2. In the terrain, north is indicated by a magnetic needle, by shadows and some dampness on boles of trees, and by the stars (an additional north).

Distance

Distances are measured in miles on the road, and versions of furlongs when in the fields of this book.

3. On a map, distance is measured by representative fraction. One distance on a Pathfinder Map is worth 25,000 similar units of distance in the terrain. The legend of the map will often have a scale which is useful for setting the points of a pair of dividers, or for checking a wheel measurer or opisometer. The dicings around map margins, make very useful measurers.

Opsiometers are wheeled rulers with many scales on them. A good way to check their readings is to run the wheel back across counted grid lines until the tool registers zero again.

4. In the terrain it is very difficult to measure distance accurately without recourse to civil engineering techniques. The best tool is the watch, given that you know your optimum walking pace. Experience shows that two hours covers five miles of walking, and the opisometer confirms this.

Pedometers look impressive, but seldom do two agree in their readings. If one instrument is preset accurately after walking around a measured track in the local park, its counting mechanism can be upset by subsequent stile clambering.

Time

Time related to Distance gives Pace. A watch becomes a useful walking tool. In this book minutes, rather than fractions of hours, are used.

5. On the map, a grid square takes fifteen minutes to cross. Directly across four squares will take an hour. A pair of dicings along the Pathfinder map margin - one blank and one lined - represents a three minute distance to walk.

6. In the terrain, bus timetables, the state of the tide, church sundials and other shadows, all help check that your watch is working correctly.

Inclination

Relief was measured, above mean sea level, in feet at a given regular interval. Contour lines were spaced 25 feet apart on the Pathfinder maps. Later the same levels were given metric labels.

Up to date maps will give metric labels to metric levels at a handy five-metre interval pattern.

7. On the map, brown contour lines depict these levels. The labels are written so the top and bottom of the numeral(s) point to the top and bottom of the hill respectively. Spot heights are frequently given off contour lines.

Some non-OS maps without height or contour numerals, have downhill-pointing lugs on the contour lines.

8. In the terrain, hills and slopes are not only visual, they can be felt so that blind people can feel the inclination of their stepping.

Some short downhill sections will be too short to show on a map, and in the damp clay of Essex good tread patterns on the boot heels are needed to combat these.

Steep terrain will have close contour lines on a map. More frequently in Essex, the contours will straggle well apart, and it is too easy to disregard them. It is their rarity which makes them valuable to maximise the changes to the horizon on any given walk.

Inclination figured strongly in the planning of the walks in this book.

Walks near
Salty Essex Estuaries

Essex has one of the longest county coastlines in England. Most of it has a wall with a nearby borrow-dyke indicating the local building material used to make the wall. It features an estuarine coastline which is a marvellous wilderness habitat of expansive inter-tidal zones. Known as *Essexcellent* estuaries, they are described in Paul Gallico's *Snowgoose* story of Dunkerque's 1941 troop rescue. Part of the territory was the backdrop to Arthur Ransome's *Secret Water*.

SALTINGS

On the sea side of the wall are the saltmarshes, mudbanks and rills where tidal forces deny too much interference by mankind. The inter-play of flora and fauna here is quite natural and vegetation is arranged in bands according to the tidal range and the salt-tolerance of plants.

BUILD UP AND DOWN

It is these salt-tolerant plants which take root between ultra high tides, that help develop the saltmarsh. When next washed by a high tide, mud settles around the plants and so helps form a slightly larger trap for more mud with the next high tide. Gradually the ooze builds to a higher level and supports a greater variety of plants and their associated fauna.

Conversely wave power can erode the fragile marsh mud away. Slight differences in the tidal force can stem from imperceptible subsidence of the land.

MAGIC

The real magic of the marshland is the music provided, free to anyone ready to listen, by redshank, oyster-catchers, and curlew and sometimes by other visitors such as Brent geese and turnstones.

ABOUT THE WALKS

There are twelve walks in this chapter. Some are down at the marshland level, as the walk profiles show. Others overlook the marshland from higher habitats. Two, overlooking the Thames are set back from the river by a former fen; and one provides a contrast by exploring a typical holiday beach.

In all cases the paths should be clearly visible on the ground and have a crop-free width of at least one metre (39 inches).

Walk 1: Wakering's Anchor

The River Roach has more estuary than freshwater length as it winds behind Southend on Sea's Thameside front. This estuary of creeks and ooze with land just poking above the high water level, may best be approached at high tide by boat, but at most tidal states footpaths from Great Wakering provide a lovely entry. Estuaries like this are rich wildernesses favoured by migrating wader-birds. The lowland walking contrasts with Walk 17 at the opposite and higher side of the county.

How to get there

From Junction 29 off the M25 travel eastwards on the A127 until it becomes the eastern end of the A13 from which the B1017 is signposted from North Shoebury. At the eastern end of Great Wakering High Street is **The Anchor** map reference 178TQ949875.

Buses   Service 4, 4A, 18 and 48 to Southend-on-Sea

Trains   Nearest station Shoeburyness on the so-called Misery
                     Line.

What is there?

Great Wakering is one of the greater village communities with shops, houses and facilities clustered shoulder to shoulder along the B1017. Pubs such as the Exhibition Inn are passed before finding The Anchor at the eastern end of High Street by the large light open space dominated by St Nicholas' church.

The Anchor holds its own against much competition and serves lunchtime snacks and M & B ales. Garden area available, and inside a collection of walking sticks to amuse walkers. Car parking space is for patrons and cars should not be left without the nod of the landlord. Alternative parking is available on Common Road verges.

Walk details

Walking distance: 7 kms (4.3 miles) needing about 105 minutes to stroll

Ordnance survey sheets   Landranger 178, The Thames Estuary

                             Pathfinder 1162 plus a few strides on 1143.

Paths used   Great Wakering 12, 13, 23, 14;Little Wakering 28, 30.

District Council   Rochford

The Walk

From the front door of the Anchor turn east along High Street towards St Nicholas' church tower and bear left on to Common Road. Pass the 4 feet deep pond and look for the transformer on stilts at the terminus of V-wiring just beyond the housing. This is the beginning of Great Wakering Common. Paths stem right and left from the bend in the road.

LT. WAKERING

POTTON ISLAND

Barlinghall Creek

track in grazing

Fleethead Creek

Fleethead Flash

Potton swing bridge

Potton Creek

track in grazing

Halfway House

Sutton Boatyard

Sutton slipway

Causeway

Wakering Reclamation Centre

Rushley Island

Common Road

Millhead Creek

Havengore Creek

Millhead Villas

re-instated arable path

Church tower in view from path worn on reclaimed land.

Gt Wakering Common

High Street

B1017

Anchor

St Nicholas' Church

GREAT WAKERING

START

WALKING DISTANCE 7 kms.

Schematic Map: not to scale

1

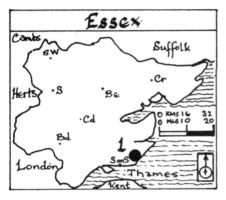

The Anchor
23 High Street
Great Wakering
SS3 0EF

☎ 0702 219265

Day	Snacks		Meals	
	Ln	Eg	Ln	Eg
Sn	✓		✓	
M	✓		✓	
T	✓		✓	
W	✓		✓	
Th	✓		✓	
F	✓		✓	
St	✓		✓	

Walk Profile

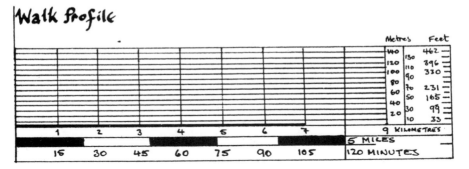

Select the left-hand one, an earthen track with gate, stile and signpost pointing northwards.

Immediately the track culverts a dyke to emphasise its causeway build-up across the lowland. Continue northwards over the crosstracks, and NNW alongside the hedge when the track swings off towards Little Wakering. The nearer churches across uninhabitated marsh are at Little Wakering and Barling.

Among the further churches to be seen is one gracing Canewdon's knoll.

Wheeling Gulls

The good field-edge path joins another causeway, at about the 5 metres-above-sea-level mark. Assume an ENE bearing and revert to NNW when on Common Road again. Wakering's Recycling Centre is on the right and the prospect of a trout farm on the left.

Where the road diffuses in to three, ignore the right fork to Sutton Boatyard, and the veering tarmac to Potton Island, in favour of the gated track by the lagoons around Halfway House **(A.950887)**.

The track continues, gradually bending northwestwards through mixed pasture and arable fields plus surface spreads of water, like permanent flood features known as fleets or flashes to join the sea-wall of tidal Fleethead Creek.

Climb the wall slowly so as to gain a view of the feeding birds before human presence disturbs them. When they have moved cautiously away, the elevation of the sea-wall enables the broader view around Barling and the Roachways.

Potton Creek

Head northwards, sloping off the wall to use another gated and stiled causeway, this one bridging Fleethead flash before merging with the sea-wall of Potton Creek. Continue at the lower level along a field-edge path with broad borrow dyke on the right-hand side, to gain access to the wall at the old fording point by the junction of creeks **(B.950902)**. This is the turnaround place.

Do not attempt to ford the Creek even at low tide for there is danger in the channel and entry to Potton Island is forbidden.

The southward sea-wall path begins the return to Great Wakering. Red shank and oyster càtchers mingle with the gulls, observant walkers may see harriers and much else. Cross the road by Potton swing-bridge. The sea-wall is further broken at Sutton Boatyard's slipway, but the path is easily rejoined to offer views down Havengore Creek to the span of Foulness Bridge from Wakering Stairs.

St Nicholas' Church Tower

Leave the sea-wall from the southwest corner of Millhead Creek **(C.954885)**, where the Recycling Centre development is again on the right-hand side. Head southwards across the grasslands towards the St Nicholas' tower top which should be in view. The next field is at a lower level and there is a decoy pond to the left of the connecting stile. The path is reinstated through the arable crop SW towards Millhead Villas.

Rejoin Common Road and face oncoming traffic for four minutes. A footpath signpost points left. Use this path and veer off on to one of several worn paths by Great Wakering Common. Overhead wires can be traced right to the V junction noticed earlier. Retrace steps along Common Road to the church and turn right on to High Street to re-locate The Anchor and its refreshing drinks.

Please leave any muddy footwear outside when you enter the pub.

Pub Yarns

Wakering is a Saxon settlement of the people of Waecer.

Sally Davy was a scullery maid at The Anchor; she went on to other posts and finished her life as Sarah Duchess of Ferrers.

Essex has about 50% of England's east coast islands. Potton, Foulness and their smaller neighbours are examples of these.

Have you noticed any marks to indicate the level of the Great Flood of 1953?

Walk 2: Tollesbury's Hope Inn

Tollesbury has an allure which draws walkers and birders, not to mention sailors and fisherfolk, back to its cul-de-sac time and time again. There are several five mile walks on offer, but not enough to experience all the moods prevalent when the sky's ever-changing light interplays with the inter-tidal ecology. Against such a backdrop thrives an attractive community at Tollesbury, with a vital link to communal affairs at The Hope.

How to get there

Leave the A12 at Kelvedon, using the B1024 to link with B1023 in Feering and then follow the B1023 in to its seaside cul-de-sac which is Tollesbury. The Hope Inn is in High Street map reference 168TL955104.

Buses	G W Osborne & Sons services from Maldon, Witham and Colchester to Tollesbury are the main connections.
Trains	Nearest station is Witham with connections via Osbornes' buses.

What is there?

Tollesbury is a large village clustered around St Mary's church and the Square on the highest part of the promontory between Old Hall Creek and the Blackwater Estuary. It is the sort of place which should figure highly in best-kept village awards if only for a good set of well-maintained parish paths. The Hope Inn is beside the B1023 entry to the village square, where another pub, the Kings Head, is located.

The Hope Inn sports some maritime features and is popular with locals and visitors alike. Greene King and Ind Coope ales served, and fresh fish features strongly on the restaurant menu. The Hope has a meeting room and offers accommodation. There is some space for cars and this is reserved for patrons. Cars should not be left there without the landlord's permission. Alternative parking is at Woodrolfe Green towards the marina.

Walk details

Walking distance	8 kms (5 miles) requiring 120 minutes to stroll
Ordnance Survey Maps	Landranger 168 Colchester & The Blackwater
	Pathfinder 1099 Witham & Tiptree (small part on 1023)
Paths used	Tollesbury 33, 19, 8, 3, 4, 5, 18, 24, 30, 31, 10, & 11
District Council	Maldon

The Walk

Use High Street's footway westward and turn left on to Elysian Gardens' footway and enter St John's Court at the southern end. A snicket between the dwellings leads to a well worn path from the back garden fences to the recreation ground left. Go right, instead on the lesser worn option to the far fence corner. Turn left on a path reinstated through the crop to a new footbridge over a deep ditch connecting with a cross track **(D.953100)**.

Red Hills

Good views across the Blackwater estuary to St Lawrence and Stone on the Dengie peninsula are usually available here. Patches of redness detected in the soil are the residues of red hills where Romans, among others, obtained salt by evaporation of sea-water.

Head westwards on the track and go right again on Prentice Hall Lane. Cross the B1023 by Garlands Farm, going right to the track by the eastern side of the buildings. Chase the gravelled track through to the first hedgerow right where a waymark points along the northern side towards Tollesbury **(E.948108)**. Use this headland, cross the double planked bridge, and where the hedge ends, follow the crop change path which bends by a mid-field pole and exits on to a bend of North Street.

Crab & Winkle Railway

Continue eastward on the footway, and where the road bends again, go left on a path sheltered by a high hedge against a garden fence. Stay beside the hedge in the ensuing paddock and be steered by hedging through to steps up and over the embankment of the former railway.

Follow the left-hand hedgeline down towards the marshes and join a path from Station Road to jointly cross the bridge left and turn right on the headland down to a cradle bridge. Repeat the manoeuvre and this time the headland connects with a ramp to the sea-wall **(F.955116.)**

The elevated walkway overlooks the vast Old Hall Creek and associated saltings, rills and fleets. This is as true a wilderness as can be found on our islands, and the birdcalls are wonderfully primeval.

Sail Lofts

Stay on the wall, initially eastwards and then serpentining all the way to Woodrolfe sail-lofts. Re-join the wall on the other side of the flood

WALKING
DISTANCE
8 kms.

RTG
136

F

headland
path

Marshes, saltings
mudflats and
rills of Old
Hall Creek

Tollesbury
Fleet

fieldedge
paths

Steps to
old railway
embankment

Carringtons

fieldedge
path

E

pole

North Rd

Garlands

B1023

START

Hope Inn

Woodrolfe
Industrial
Estate

G

Woodrolfe
Hard

Pool

Marina

St Mary's
Church

Woodrolfe
Farm

Prentice
Hall
Lane

re-instated
arable
path

D

Recreation
Ground

midfield path

Mell Road

TOLLESBURY

Schematic Map: not to scale

2

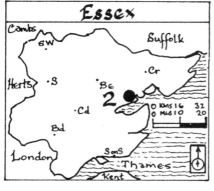

The Hope Inn
16 High Street
Tollesbury
CM9 8RG

☎ 0621
869238

Day	Snacks		Meals	
	Lh	Eg	Lh	Eg
Sn	✓		✓	
M				
T				
W				
Th				
F				
St	✓			

Walk Profile

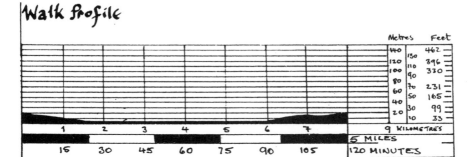

defence buttresses **(G.966106)**. Pass the pool and the marina and leave the wall just before the stile above the south-eastern corner of the marina. Use the ramp descending by lagoons and swinging right to link with Woodrolfe Farm Lane.

Leave the marshland levels via the Lane and pass the black weather-boarded farm buildings richly capped with red pantiles to join the tarmac of Mell Road. Go left by the telephone kiosk and leave the speed restrictions behind to find a crossing of paths at a grand vantage point to look across the estuary at Bradwell more than a mile away.

Cage

Go right and fork right at the first stile/gate and exit on to Church Street which leads via the fine square tower of St Mary's church and the nearby cage to Tollesbury Square. Go left by the Kings Head to enter High Street and return to The Hope Inn. Please remove muddy footwear before entering the Inn.

Pub Yarns

The former crab and winkle railway line heralded new life for Tollesbury which was never sustained. The trains took an hour to cover the ten miles to the junction with the main line at Kelvedon. The pier, a wooden structure, stretched way out to the deep water channel in the estuary. It was abandoned and then partially destroyed during World War II, and the Great Flood of 1953 finished the destruction.

During World War II an Ack Ack gun and searchlight stations were situated near Mell Creek and these attracted an unsuccessful bombing raid.

Walk 3: Oakley's Maybush

Great Oakley has not over-expanded in population, as so many Essex villages have done during the great intensification of dwellings around the Capital since World War II. This is to Great Oakley's advantage. It retains its village status on a ridge overlooking Hamford Water and Dovercourt Bay, each house a bastion against cruel winter winds from the Urals. This walk can be bracing at times, and is always filled with interest along the ridge.

How to get there

From the A12 trunk road select the A120 Harwich Road eastwards from the Ardleigh interchange. Drive to Ramsey roundabout with the B1352. Go right and right again on to Mayes Lane, and right yet again on the B1414 which leads to the square of Great Oakley centre. The Maybush is just in Farm Road, map reference 169TM196275.

Buses	102, and 104 Harwich to Colchester by Eastern National.
Trains	Nearest station is Dovercourt Bay with bus connection.

What is there?

The central space created by a squared opening in the building line of Great Oakley's High Street is beset by the parish war memorial. Here too Farm Road and Queen Street form an attractive junction with the B1414. The Maybush is a real village pub also well-known to walkers from many local rambling clubs for its Adnams ales. Snacks are available occasionally. There is no pub parking. Street parking is by the war memorial with the overflow along the road to Harwich.

Walk details

Walking distance	7 kms (4.6 miles) needing about 105 minutes to stroll
Ordnance Survey maps	Landranger 169 Ipswich & The Naze
	Pathfinder 1078 Walton on the Naze
Paths used	Great Oakley 8, 20, 17, 16, 15, 13, 11, 12.
	Little Oakley 13, 11, 3. Ramsey 27, 26.
District Council	Tendring

The Walk

Walk south-eastwards along Farm Road for about 3 minutes to get beyond Back Lane and the last house on the left-hand side and to locate the first footpath signpost pointing left. The path follows a bi-concrete strip through fields dedicated to growing vegetables. Eventually the track bends left to follow the curve of a hedgeline towards the housing of Harwich Road.

RAMSEY

White house

Wayside

Rectory Road

change-crop line path

Saltwater Bridge

The Soils

clear midfield paths

LITTLE OAKLEY

Little Oakley Hall

cemetery

South House Farm

Stepover ditch

fieldedge path

Great Oakley Hall

B1414

re-instated midfield path with fieldedge diversion

START

Maybush

re-instated arable path

Farm Road

WALKING DISTANCE 7kms

Lodge Farm

B1414

GREAT OAKLEY

Schematic Map: not to scale   RTG 137   ③

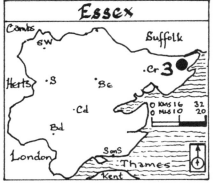

The Maybush

Farm Road

Great Oakley

CO12 5B

☎ 0255
886183

Day	Snacks		Meals	
	LN	Eg	LN	Eg
Sn				
M	✓	✓		
T	✓	✓		
W	✓	✓		
Th	✓	✓		
F	✓	✓		
St				

Walk Profile

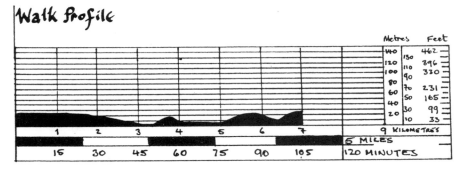

The footpath leaves the track in favour of maintaining a straighter line reinstated through the crops. This end of the path has been subject to re-alignment proposals and should these come in to force, the new line is likely to be along the track and then by the inside of the Harwich Road hedge as far as the north-eastern corner of the field.

Hamford Water

Face oncoming traffic along the B1414 as far as the sharp bend by Great Oakley Hall. Cross to the stile by the metallic gate and walk the headland, still on a NE bearing, bypassing the Hall's farmyard and enjoying views over Hamford Water from the Oakley ridge path.

By-pass the south-eastern side of the cemetery where the former church is now a dwelling and maintain direction on a grassy track until the path junction at the rear of Little Oakley Hall is reached **(H.214285)**.

Descend from the low ridge on a properly reinstated path NNW to the dip of a pond and a stand of trees. Chicane left right through the trees to exit via a stile and another mid-field path NNW out to White House. Turn left for a few paces along Rectory Road and turn right before Wayside.

Saltwater Bridge

The fieldgate-with-stile is set back from the road. Good views across to Ramsey's church and windmill, and beyond to churches across the Stour in Suffolk, may be seen from the ensuing path before it dips by the right-hand hedge in to the valley of Ramsey Brook.

A double-gated bridge of the brook has double side stiles sometimes unsighted under ungrazed vegetation **(J.208294)**. Join a brookside path when on the Ramsey side, going SSE to leave the grazing field by an improvised stile and following the field fringe, under the trees, to a small paddock by Saltwater Bridge. Squeeze between brook and paddock and a stile provides the exit to the road.

Uphill right a T-junction of roads is converted to a crossing with the inclusion, of the footpath. A change-crop alignment in the arable acres steers the path westwards to the parish boundary **(K.202291)**. A short hedge on the hilltop further steers it WSW and then a selection from many sets of tractor wheel-marks radiating from South House Farm can be made across to the steading. Beware of reversing vehicles when walking through the farmyard to join the road by the pond.

Oakley Ridge

Downhill the road bends sharply left. The footpath goes equally sharply right. At the end of the SE hedgeline dip southwards to the far corner of the field. Often a diversion around the lower field-edge is in operation, and it is necessary to step over the ditch for access to the next brookside field. Continue SE ignoring footbridges carrying other paths up to Great Oakley.

Join the gravelled drive from Lodge Farm by its bridge over the brook. Turn right uphill by the reservoirs and approach Lodge Farm buildings.

About 70 metres before they are reached **(L.191282)**, a yellow arrow points to a reinstated path down to the brook. Use this one which has a good bridge at the bottom and a sound path up the other side of the valley, to emerge between cottage gardens on to High Street.

Conclude the walk with a small diversion. Go right along High Street to the shop, cross to enter Back Lane and within a few paces turn left on to Queen Street. This street of charming rooflines leads back to The Maybush.

Villagers are used to seeing ramblers' muddy footwear stacked neatly near the door. Please do not walk through the pub depositing large clumps of clay on the carpet.

Pub Yarns

When this area was a forest, oak trees were dominant. These gave two local villages their names, and provided ship builders of Harwich with timber.

The several islands of Hamford Water behind the tower of Walton on the Naze, were the backdrop for Arthur Ransome's story Secret Waters.

Excavations at St Mary's church, Little Oakley confirmed occupation of the site for a thousand years. The present building is a domestic dwelling and the living is now shared with Ramsey.

The secret sea-wall factory attracts many rumours about danger.

Walk 4: Mersea Island's Fox Inn

The former West Mersea urban district council now has a parish council like East Mersea, except its chairperson has the title of Mayor. Estate Agents flourish on Mersea Island for it is a desirable place to live. It is also a very popular recreation island for all manner of sea sports. Sometimes on a hot summer Sunday with the prospect of a midday high tide, it seems the island will sink under the weight of vehicles crossing the Strood.

Importantly Mersea Island is positioned at the orifice of the huge double Blackwater and Colne estuary. The shipping lanes are not so busy now, but Trinity House Pilots still operate in both rivers. The great mudflats exposed at low tide are part of the Colne Estuary National Nature Reserve.

How to get there

Slip off the A12 trunk road on to roads signed (A134) at Lexden near Colchester. Connect with the A604 and then with the A134 dual carriageway which leads up the hill of Colchester and then eastwards across Southway to Town station roundabout. Join the B1025 and follow it across The Strood causeway on to Mersea Island. Immediately fork left for East Mersea, and take the first right, Dawes Lane, through to the crossroads. The Fox is a few metres east along East Road, map reference 168TM025135.

Buses	West Mersea - West Bergholt services 67 and 76
Trains	Both Colchester North and Town stations served by above buses.

What is there?

The Cross is a junction of residential roads near the centre of the island and with a pub nearby. Wherever the action is, on or around the island, you can get to it from The Fox. This is a friendly freehouse, well equipped to serve local residents and "passing trade" with Adnams, Greene King and other good ales. There is a restaurant, meeting room and garden plus some space for parking patrons' cars. Cars should not be left there without the agreement of the landlord. Alternative parking on verge approaching East Mersea church.

Walk details

Walking distance	7.5 kms (4.8 miles) needing 112 minutes to stroll
Ordnance Survey maps	Landranger 168 Colchester & The Blackwater; Pathfinder 1100 Bradwell and Mersea Island
Paths used	West Mersea 26,16, East Mersea 1, 5, 4, 8.
District Council	Colchester

The Walk

Head westwards from the Fox along East Road to The Cross and turn south on to Cross Lane, a gated lane with squeeze stiles leading down via the Treatment Works to the beach east of Southview beach huts. Walk the beach eastwards and if necessary, because of the state of the tide, join the wall-top path by the old blockhouse **(M.032125)**.

Birds of The Mudflats

The earthen sea-wall path runs along by the Waldegrave lagoons and across the apex of the boat launching ramps from the caravan park. Ignore inland paths by the trees and buildings of the County Council's camping site for schools and youth groups, and join the concrete section of the sea-wall. A flight of concrete steps leads up from the beach.

Onward March

Locked gates and stiles prevent motor-cyclists from weaving amid promenaders, and perversely also bar paraplegic wheelchair-bound persons from the seaward gaze of this fine section. Inland the view is graced by the greystone tower of St Edmund the Martyr's church.

Coopers Beach caravan park is the next cluster of buildings, the first of which is the shop **(N.052136)**. Leave the wall by the ramp and head inland towards the church on a track by a recreational area. Merge with the camp road and share the exit by the church.

Turn left by the tank on pillars, use the stile beside the gate and gain access to the westward leading headland with hedge and overhead wires on the left-hand side.

Rewsalls

A culvert bridge carries the path in to the second big field. A footbridge connects with the third field, where the path is reinstated beneath the wires and through the arable crop to a road bend by Rewsalls Farm pond. Leave all buildings on the left-hand side, going northwards for a few paces on the road before resuming the westward mode on another mid-field path.

WEST MERSEA   EAST MERSEA

START

East Road

Barn Cottage

re-instated arable path

St Edmunds Church

fieldedge paths

Fox

To Waldegraves

Rewsalts

Brierley

Re-instated path (arable)

Cross Lane

private road public footpath

Coot

Fox

WALKING DISTANCE 7·5 kms

Coopers Beach Shop

borrow dyke

beach   earthen wall   Concrete wall

Nature Reserve

Mersea Mudflats at Low tide

(4)

Schematic Map: not to scale

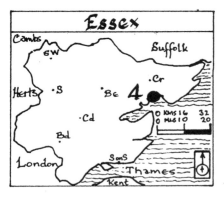

The Fox Inn

East Road

West Mersea

CO5 8SA

0206
383391

Day	Snacks		Meals	
	Ln	Eg	Ln	Eg
Sn	✓		✓	
M	✓		✓	
T	✓	✓	✓	✓
W	✓	✓	✓	✓
Th	✓	✓	✓	✓
F	✓	✓	✓	✓
St	✓	✓	✓	✓

Walk Profile

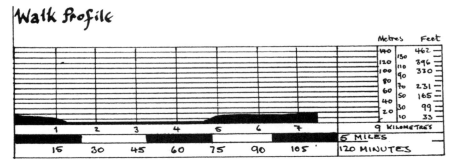

Slatted Bridge

This one dips to a slatted footbridge connecting with the fifth field. The left-hand hedge-following routine comes back in to action through this and the next field, until the path merges with the West Barn Cottage drive.

Continue westwards beyond the junction with Waldegraves Road and join East Road at a bend. Turn westwards again and face the oncoming traffic by the 30 speed sign and back to The Fox and its refreshing ales.

Please remove muddy footwear before entering this or any other pub.

Pub Yarns

A former incumbent for ten years from 1871 at East Mersea church was the Rev. Sabine Baring-Gould. He was also a poet, collector of folk songs, novelist and biographer. He gave us the novels *Mehalah* and *Richard Cable* about the 19th century life around Mersea saltings, and the hymn *Onward Christian Soldiers*.

Oysters from Pyefleet are acclaimed from afar, but their harvests have been less successful since the prolonged cold of winter 1962.

Sail making and yachting still dominate activity at Mersea Hard.

The re-building of the shed on Packing Marsh Island has won a prestigious award.

Mersea Barrow, today much smaller than it was even in Baring-Gould's time, was probably built by a British chief for a very important Roman lady.

At the eastern end of the island, not reached by this walk, is Cudmore Grove Country Park.

Walk 5: Manningtree's Skinners' Arms

Manningtree is another Essex waterside settlement where sea-related activity is so clustered as to tantalise land-lubbers. Few settlements can be more curious than this one. Manningtree has some features of a small town yet it is the smallest civil parish area in Essex. Manningtree school and Manningtree railway station are both in Lawford. Both parishes are interlocked with Mistley.

It is Mistley which provides both the architectural glamour and the thriving industry alongside the tidal sweep of the Stour estuary today. It is a place worth investigating and it provides good footpaths from which to make lead-free inspections.

How to get there

Leave the A12 for the B1070 through East Bergholt on the Suffolk side of Dedham Vale. At Cattawade turn right on the A137, cross the Stour and negotiate the railway crossing (level or under options) to reach a roundabout at the bottom of Cox's Hill in Lawford.

Turn left on to the B1352 here and pass under another railway arch to locate The Skinners' Arms by the parish boundary where Station Road becomes High Street by the junction which serves as a market place, map reference 169TM104319.

What is there?

Manningtree's market place is by a junction of six roads, with conveniences, plus some new flats and a supermarket, bus stops and a pub.

The Skinners' Arms is a friendly local pub with a range of bar snacks. It serves Tolly Cobbold and Courage ales. The limited car parking is augmented by a much larger 4 hour car-park located behind the pub. The entrance is off Riverside Road East.

Buses	Colchester Harwich services 102, 103, 104 Eastern National. Ipswich Mistley services 94 Eastern Counties
Trains	Manningtree Station. (junction for Harwich)

WALK DETAILS

Walking distance	6.6 kms (4.1 miles) requiring 100 minutes to stroll
Ordnance Survey maps	Landrangers 169 Ipswich & The Naze; 168 Colchester & The Blackwater; Pathfinder 1053 Manningtree and Dedham
Paths used	Mistley 15, 16, 4, 23, 1. Lawford 1, 2, 3, 4.
District Council	Tendring

The Walk

From the front door of the Skinners' Arms turn left along High Street's sidewalk beyond the zebra crossing. Turn left and swing right with Quay Street to merge with Manningtree's short beach behind The

Crown. The sea-wall gives way to a greensward as Manningtree gives way to Mistley.

Known as The Walls, this walk with a choice of tarmac or grass alongside the B1352 road, overlooks the mudflats of Seafield Bay at low tide, but the swans will not overlook your passing without a begging glance. Hopping Bridge, over the outfall stream from the Environmental Centre's lake, is a popular place for the swan feeding.

Mistley Thorn

A little further on is a Robert Adam creation, Mistley's twin towers. A path squeezes between the towers' compound and Portishead House to Rigby Quay.

Stay upside of the quayside watchful of reversing vehicles, to pass south of the Craft workshops and the Swan fountain, again a legacy of Robert Adam's design. The upstairs coffee shop of the Craft Centre is worth a visit, as is the Hotel.

Pump

Cross carefully to The Green beside The Thorn Hotel. Pass the pump and turn left around the Anchorage 1898. A permissive path connects with the rightful path towards the E D M E's silo area. Go right from the silo, cross a footbridge and use some steps to get to the tunnel level under the railway line.

From the railway head S across the pasture parallel with the edge of School Wood left to join Shrublands Road by a gas marker **(Q.116314)**. Turn left to cross the cinder topped bridge and rise by Inglenook to reach an entrance to Furze Hill Playing Fields. Enter here and skirt the pylon's compound to get to the eastern fence by the rugby hut. Follow the fence S to join the Mistley Heath path by Furze Hill Wood **(R.121310)**.

Green Lane

Go right downhill by the playing field fence to the stile beyond the lake.

Downhill a little further is a bridge amid grazing land with a footbridge south of it. Use the wider bridge and climb the worn path up the slope

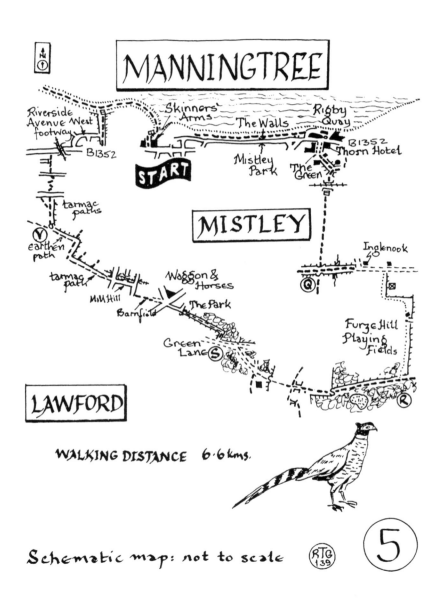

MANNINGTREE

Riverside Avenue West footway
B1352

Skinners' Arms
The Walls
Rigby Quay
B1352
Thorn Hotel
Mistley Park
The Green

START

tarmac paths

earthen path

tarmac path

Mill Hill
Barnfield

Waggon & Horses
The Park

Green Lane

MISTLEY

Inglenook

Furze Hill Playing Fields

LAWFORD

WALKING DISTANCE 6·6 kms.

Schematic map: not to scale

5

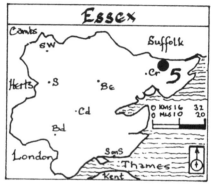

Skinners' Arms

High Street

Manningtree

CO11 1A

☎   0206
      393658

Day	Snacks		Meals	
	Ln	Eg	Ln	Eg
Sn		✓		
M	✓	✓		
T	✓	✓		
W	✓	✓		
Th	✓	✓		
F	✓	✓		
St	✓	✓		

Walk Profile

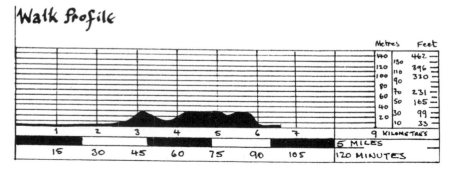

to a gate and stile by Dairy House Farm. Keep the farmstead on the left-hand side and join its drive to merge with Green Lane by the corner of the kennels' link-fencing. Bear left W and within 2 minutes turn right at a path junction **(S.110313)**.

Barnfield

Fences steer this path through to the dwellings of The Park and out to a fork after crossing New Road by the Waggon & Horses. Select Barnfield which becomes a path through to the Evangelical church. Go right to the red mail box and left on to Mill Hill. Dip to the Tendring Hundred Waterworks and rise to carefully cross Colchester Road on the western side of the valley. A tarmac path begins by Riverview open space and continues between schools and housing, with a discontinuous water-proof surface to a stile above Cotman Avenue **(V.098318)**.

Smallest Parish

Turn northwards to cross the Avenue and descend the zigzag path over Gainsborough Drive down to Station Road. Go right under the railway arch, and left on to the sidewalk of Riverside Avenue West. A footpath beside fencing which separates the road from Riverside Avenue East, is used left to get access to the sea-wall of the Stour Estuary.

Gently ascend the steps to see the birds before they see you. Turn right on the walltop path to re-enter Manningtree, the smallest parish in the county, and leave the wall via a flight of steps down to the car-park behind The Skinners' Arms. The exit path is beside The Health Centre. And now, after changing to clean shoes, for some healthy refreshment!

Pub Yarns

Some say Mistley quayside, indebted to Richard Rigby and Son, should be called Mistley Thorn to separate it from Mistley Heath, the original inland settlement. The son, also Richard, was Paymaster General to George III and he extended his father's ambitions for a Spa town by building a shipyard, quays, a lime kiln and creating a timber yard.

Associated with this area is Matthew Hopkins, notorious 17th century Witchfinder General who was responsible for the death of almost 200 women.

E D M E is English Diastatic Malt Extract.

St Michael's and All Angels church at Manningtree needed a huge sum of money to restore the building in 1964. St.Mary's church in Mistley had just received a similar huge sum for restoration work. The two congregations merged to use St.Mary's. Church ruins at Mistley Heath are evidence of a similar merger at an earlier date.

Thomas Tusser (1515 - 80) introduced the growing of barley to this area. His FIVE HUNDRED POINTS OF GOOD HUSBANDRY is still read today.

Motorists pull up along The Walls to feed the swans which appear content to be at a neck's length from humans and their shiny machines.

Walk 6: Maldon's Welcome Sailor

Situated fairly central to Essex, Maldon is a port by virtue of being the bridging place across one of the big estuaries indenting England's east coast. Both the rivers Chelmer and Blackwater meet at Maldon to share the estuary, and a canal breaches the gap between the rivers to create a local beauty spot known as Beeleigh Falls.

The Welcome Sailor is located on the sea-wall beside that initial bridge and from it a popular walk ensues through to Curling Tye Green and back.

How to Get There

Maldon is at the terminus of the A414 road from Hertfordshire through junction 7 of the M11 and the Chelmsford intersection of the A12 dual carriageway. Use the northern by-pass of Maldon and turn towards the town along the B1018 to find the Welcome Sailor alongside Fullbridge at the foot of Market Hill, map reference 168TL851074.

Buses	Colchester - Maldon 119 route. Chelmsford - Maldon 91/2 route
Trains	Nearest station - Hatfield Peverel with bus 91/2 connections

What is there?

Fullbridge is an attractive road bridge spanning the Chelmer estuary, with remnant evidence of milling, wine importing and timber trading behind the recreational boating now on the seaward side. Grassy banks contrast the view on the inland side, and facing steep Market Hill over the bridge are the warm red tiles of The Welcome Sailor. Swans and ducks will dip for any pub food spared from the beer garden tables between river wall and path 11. The pub is complete with garden, meeting room and children's room, and meals are available as specified. Car parking is limited and for patrons only, entrance via Mill Lane. Vehicles should not be left without the landlord's permission. Alternative parking space can be found near Great Beeleigh's London Road bend verge.

Walk details

Walking distance	8 kms (5 miles); requires about 120 minutes to stroll
Ordnance Survey maps	Landranger 168 Colchester & The Blackwater
	Pathfinder sheet 1123 Maldon
Paths used	Maldon 37, 4, 3, 19, 47, 25, 11, 44.
	Woodham Walter 29, 28.
District Council	Maldon

The Walk

Cross the river to the bottom of Market Hill and turn right on to path 37 to walk the sea-wall upstream until the path turns up some steps and joins Cromwell Lane. A stile at the end of the lane admits the path to a

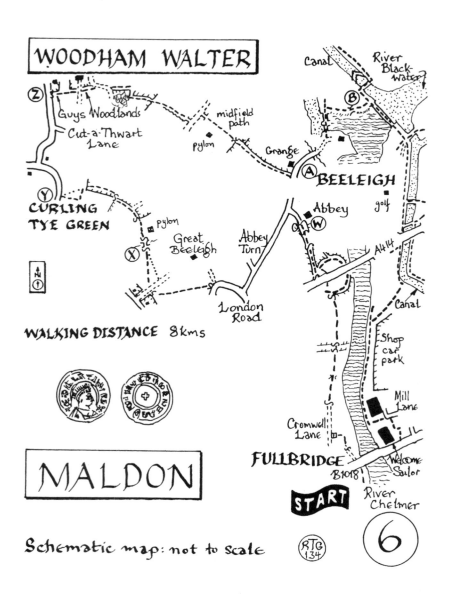

WOODHAM WALTER

Canal   River Black-water

Guys Woodlands

Cut-a-Thwart Lane

midfield path

pylon

Grange

B

A BEELEIGH

CURLING TYE GREEN

Abbey   golf

Great Beeleigh   Abbey Turn   W

pylon   A414

London Road

Canal

WALKING DISTANCE 8kms

Shop car park

Mill Lane

Cromwell Lane

MALDON

FULLBRIDGE   Welcome Sailor

B1018

START   River Chelmer

Schematic map: not to scale   RTG 134   6

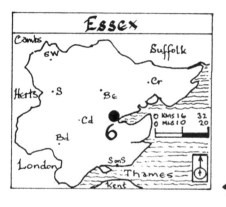

Welcome Sailor

1 Fullbridge

Maldon

CM9 7LD

☎ 0621 852167

Day	Snacks		Meals	
	Lh	E6	Lh	E6
Sn	✓		✓	
M	✓		✓	
T	✓		✓	
W	✓		✓	
Th	✓		✓	
F	✓		✓	
St	✓		✓	

Walk Profile

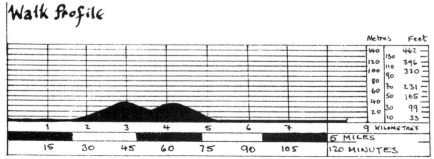

double grazing patch where the path contours the riverbank as far as the A414 bridge.

Loop right under the road bridge and continue on the hard-surfaced path until above road level on the other side. Turn right on to Lovers' Lane, passing the pylon and climbing the lower stile to enter two more patches of grazing before joining Beeleigh Chase which passes the gateway to Beeleigh Abbey. **(W.839077)**.

Great Beeleigh

Rise left from the valley up Abbey Turn, ignore Cut-a-Thwart Lane and turn right to face oncoming traffic along London Road. From the first bend, a track branches off to Great Beeleigh Farm, and a stile indicates a path aligned between road and track. It is reinstated WSW across to a back garden fence where an exit stile connects with an orchard. The cordons are not aligned with the right-of-way, but by moving along the track right half a dozen rows, an easy route to the double stiled footbridge is found **(X.831071)**.

Cut-A-Thwart Lane

Climb the slope of the grazing plot and enter the upper grassland to walk with hedge on right-hand side as far as the corner stile. Swap sides of the hedge and from the next corner, cross the narrow neck of arable land to the gateway and finger post on Curling Tye Lane **(Y. 824070)**.

Turn right and right again at Curling Tye Green to pass High Oaks. Again ignore Cut-a-Thwart Lane to use Manor Road as an approach to Guy's Farm. Path 28 starts from the pole at the nearest garden corner **(Z. 822078)**, and continues across the field to the southern fence of Woodlands' garden. Cross the drive and after the garden, join the farmland track heading by the northern side of the spinney.

Rivers Meet

The track finishes at a fieldbridge right. The path maintains the same direction now with ditch on left-hand side to the corner bridge. In to the next field continue for a score of paces before reaching a ditch source.

Steer by the left-hand side of it to connect with the bridge on to the track.

Descend in the valley for another score of paces along the track. Turn right over a double-planked bridge to join a reinstated path across an arable field and under pyloned wires. Connect with a culvert bridge and continue with hedge on left-hand side out to the lane by Grange Farm **(A.839078)**.

Go left downhill. The lane becomes an unmade road as far as Beeleigh Mill and then pedestrians continue through the metallic stile to bridge over the sluice retaining Chelmer waters to canal level. Turn right off the further end of the footbridge and pick a path around to the stile by Speeny Lockgates **(B.840084)**.

Ignore the footbridge over the canal and go right on the path atop the sluices retaining Blackwater waters to the required level.

Canal Towpath

Join the Golf Club drive off Langford bridge and walk the canal towpath beyond Chapman Bridge and underpass the A414 to reach the car-park fence of a supermarket. Turn right alongside the fence and mount the sea-wall of tidal Chelmer Reach.

Go downstream to enter the beer garden of the Welcome Sailor. Please replace or cover any muddy footwear before entering the pub.

Pub Yarns

During the reign of Aethelstan 925 - 939, coins were made at Maldon's mint.

In 1991 Maldon celebrated the Millenium of the Song of the Battle of Maldon when the Viking invaders defeated the Saxon army led by Bryhtnoth.

The Maldon Crystal Salt Company, near Fullbridge, still produces table salt, a much acclaimed export, by extraction from sea-water.

Beeleigh Abbey was founded in 1180 by Robert de Mantell for a Premonstratensian order of Monks. The building now houses a library belonging to the family of the famous London bookshop, Foyles.

Alfred Sadd was a Maldon missionary working in the Gilbert and Ellis Islands when he perished at the time of the Japanese occupation in World War II.

Walk 7: Langdon Hill's Crown

Laindon's fine ridge of wood and grassland overlooking the Thames estuary is now part of Basildon and much of the ridge has Country Park status. The Park is in two parts, Westley Heights by The Crown, and Langdon Hills East around One Tree Hill, a hill with one tree recurring many times. Both areas are popular for orienteers' training, being small zones in which it is easy to re-locate one's position. One necessary aspect of marshland or estuary walking is that one seldom gets an overview of the terrain underfoot. This walk offers that more general view, and couples it to an industrialised scene, for that is an important part of Essex too.

How to Get There

From Junction 30 leave the M25 and select the A13 east to seek the interchange with the A1014 at Horndon-on-the-Hill. Little B1007 shares the same junction before going northwards up to the trees of Westley Heights. Pass Langdon Hills church and find The Crown perched on the hilltop - the highest pub before the North Pole - just as the South Hill carriageway doubles and is re-named Staneway, map reference 178TQ681867.

What is there?

The large Inn shares a wooded hilltop situation with the Country Park entrance, and the Dry Street junction by St Mary's church. The views northward are over part of Basildon's suburbia to the catchment landscapes of Mar Dyke and the Rivers Wid and Crouch. To the south, beyond the Thames-side oil and gas industry sites, are the North Downs of Kent.

The Crown serves Ind Coope, Tetley and Young's ales, has a garden and a good range of bar food. It also has a large car-park to match its popular status. Cars should not be left there without the landlord's permission. Alternative car parking is available at both Country Parks.

Buses services 31, 32, 241, 244 & 273 Basildon

Trains Laindon or Basildon stations

Walk details

Walking distance	5 kilometres (3.1 miles) needing about 75 minutes to stroll
Ordnance Survey maps	Landrangers 177 East London;178 The Thames Estuary. Pathfinder1161 Basildon
Paths used	Country Park paths and permissive New Town development paths in Basildon
District Council	Basildon

The Walk

A wooded drive bounds the southern side of The Crown car-park. Use this drive to gain entry to Westley Heights Country Park. Head ENE

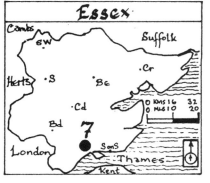

The Crown
High Road
Langdon Hills
Basildon
Essex.

☎ 0268
414233

Day	Snacks		Meals	
	L	ES	L	ES
Sn	✓		✓	
M	✓	✓	✓	
T	✓	✓	✓	
W	✓	✓	✓	
Th	✓	✓	✓	
F	✓	✓	✓	
St	✓	✓	✓	

Walk Profile

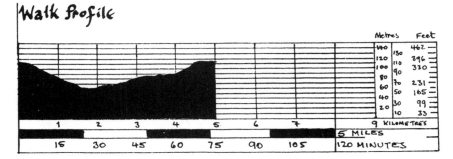

from the convenience block, to cross the car-park and pass the information hut and a copper-beech tree to stay on the grassy ridge of Rungals Meadow. The pathway is mown and has intermittent shrubbery on the left-hand side. Pass a pond right, and descend slightly towards an exit stile south of the white boarded Westley Hall.

Kingston Hill

Let the hedges steer to a junction with Homestead Drive by a slate roofed out building **(C.685869)**. Go right along the wooded drive and keep left at the fork with Southway. Overhead wires guide the way up Kingston Hill. Just over the crest, the track clearly bears left sloping down to the town centre NE. This is the orthodox route, turning right on The Bridleway S to One Tree Hill. But other stiles in the vicinity pose problems of choice. An interesting short cut appears well-worn through probable former plotlands.

The Chase

For the short-cut, select the stile allowing the eastward progress to continue, and walk under trees with a stream on the right-hand side forming a border with grassland. Pass a pond and serpentine on paths to the stiled exit on to The Chase. Use The Chase southwards for a couple of minutes to find a stile left. In this plot too, paths serpentine through the scrubland bushes, and a generally eastward direction is maintained to locate the exit stile on to The Bridleway **(D.693870)**.

One Tree Hill

Turn southward again and chase the bridleway through to its junction with Dry Street. Cross to One Tree Hill with care. There is a pedestrians' route off the western side. Pass the Memorial Inter-denominational church before crossing to a sidewalk which is on the safer side of the hedge. Stay parallel with the road, cross the vehicular entrance to Martinhole Wood, dip down and climb up the Country Park grassland slopes, to find a gap in the hedge by a pond nestling in the road's chicane.

Langdon Hills East car-park, Information Centre, conveniences etc. are across the road **(E.696860)**. Head westwards up the steps by the copper-beech tree and follow the worn path around to the AA viewing platform.

Leave this vantage point southwards, veering right with the fence line to resume westward progress on an undulating path with occasional sightings of The Mount hospital fence-line.

Other paths converge to form a well worn track dipping towards a gentle bend to the right above the slopes of Northland Wood. Climb with the northward path under the canopy of trees to find an exit stile on to a bridleway. Continue northwards on the gravelled track to re-join Dry Street by Clapgate Cottage.

Westley Heights

Walk the grassy verge westwards along busy narrow Dry Street as far as Well Green Cottage **(F.685864)**. Path 176 passes west side of the garden and the ensuing drive to find a stiled entrance to Westley Heights (Langdon Hills West) Country Park.

Back in an area of mown strips, select one going left of the stand of trees, by the westward-steering fence as far as the stile where the grassland begins to give way to woodland. Turn right to keep the trees of Combe Wood on the left and the information hut comes back in to view. Retrace steps westward to the B1007 and refreshment at The Crown. Please wear only non-muddy shoes in the pub.

Pub Yarns

Langdon Hills is the long hill of Laindon. Here the Country Park habitats attract butterflies, and butterflies will attract lepidopterists to study butterfly wild life. Will the oak trees of Coombe Wood attract the rare Purple Emperor?

Laindon's plotlands stemmed from the implementation of an old philosophy of making homes fit for heroes home from the battles. People migrated to them from London. Some plots reverted to shrub and woodland when neglected by original owners' successors.

The new church of St.Mary's church has been coupled with All Saints church down the hill since 1876.

Near The Crown, a beacon functioned in 1588 to warn of the invasion.

Walk 8: Herongate's Olde Dog Inn

The headwaters of Mar Dyke gather around West and East Horndon, to flow across Orsett Fen where they quickly lose impetus from the heights of Herongate before contributing to the Thames by Aveley. The views are surprisingly rural for a location so close to London's Thameside and the M25.

This walk offers these views of estuarine Essex from an ancient inn and a part of Thorndon Country Park known as Halfway House. By Stoneyhill Wood, golfers awaiting their swing on the golf course - and walkers waiting to cross a fairway in use - can relax by overviewing the shipping along Tilbury Hope.

How to get there

From the M25 Junction 29 use the A127 eastwards to the Halfway House interchange with the A128. Turn northwards for one mile. Turn eastwards on Billericay Road. Within three-quarters of a mile find The Olde Dog Inn on a bend of the road, map reference 177TQ642910.

Buses	Services 151 & 265 via Herongate church
Trains	West Horndon station with 265 connections weekdays
	Laindon station with 151 connections weekdays

What is there?

Billericay Road has cottages fronting arable fields and occasional woods. The low-eaved 500 year-old pub also houses La Piccola Italia Restaurant and sells a range of CAMRA approved ales. Extensive views can be seen from the pub garden across the fen to the tidal Thames. There are car parking spaces for use with landlord approval. Alternative parking is at Halfway House Country Park.

Walk details

Walking distance	6.8 kms (4.3 miles) needing about 100 minutes. to stroll
Ordnance Survey maps	Landranger 177 East London
	Pathfinder 1142 Billericay and 1161 Basildon
Paths used	Herongate 60, 59, 41,
District Council	Brentwood

The Walk

A track off the road bend leads southwards from the Inn. Fork right by the pub hedge and enter the small paddock to turn to the exit stile along the left-hand hedge. The path across to the northwest corner of Dog Wood is diverted via the right-hand hedge and then takes the shortest route across to the stand of coppiced trees. Halfway along the woodland edge a waymark points right.

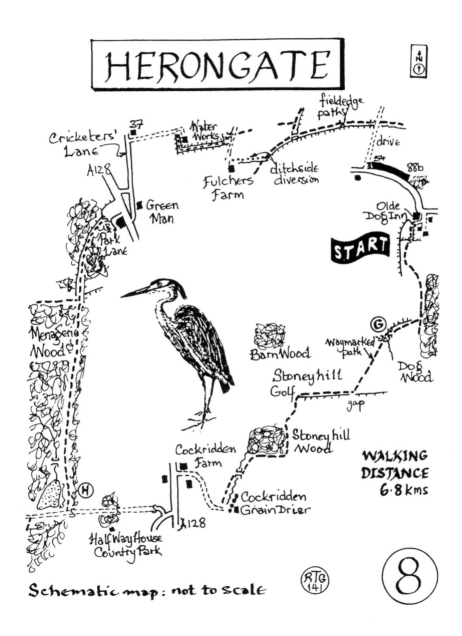

HERONGATE

fieldedge paths

drive

Cricketers' Lane
37
Water Works
A128
Green Man
Park Lane

Fulchers Farm
ditchside diversion

54
88b

Olde Dog Inn

START

Menagerie Wood

Barn Wood
Stoneyhill Golf
G
Waymarked path
Dog Wood
gap

Cockridden Farm
Stoneyhill Wood

WALKING DISTANCE 6·8 kms

H

Cockridden Grain Drier

Half Way House Country Park
A128

Schematic map: not to scale

RTG 141

⑧

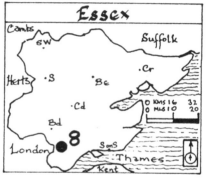

The Olde **Dog Inn**

Billericay Road

Herongate

CM13 3SD

☎ 0277
      810337

Day	Snacks		Meals	
	Ln	Eg	Ln	Eg
Sn	✓	✓		
M	✓	✓	✓	✓
T	✓	✓	✓	✓
W	✓	✓	✓	✓
Th	✓	✓	✓	✓
F	✓	✓	✓	✓
St	✓	✓	✓	✓

Walk Profile

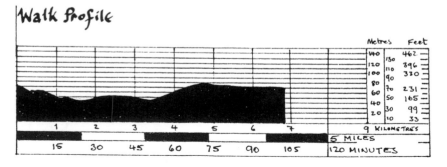

Follow this to gain a hedge on the right-hand side and a set of footbridges in the corner **(G.642906)**. Cross the ditches and head south-wards along a swath of the golf course to the gap in the southern hedgeline. Turn right with hedge on left-hand side and from the end join the track passing east and south sides of Stoneyhill Wood. The track continues from the trees alongside a hedge and swaps sides over a cartbridge to progress beside a young Mar Dyke to a silo-stand at Cockridden grain drier.

Country Park

Go right on the track by Cockridden Farm to the greenswards of the A128. Cross carefully and head southwards to find the entrance to the Country Park. Use the drive westwards by the information and convenience block to pass through Octagon Plantation and then on grassland descend to the Mill Wood trees.

Immediately under the canopy of trees, leave the main track in favour of one of the minor paths going right. These converge above the lake **(H.628900)** and head northwards just in the eastern fringe of the woodland. The pathway is quite delightful, more a chain of woodland glades. A path from Childerditch joins the path by the northern end of Menagerie Wood. Fences and woodland banks steer the path out to Park Lane and the A128.

Cricketers' Lane

Across the junction with Cricketers' Lane is the Green Man. Turn left as far as 37 Cricketers' Lane, and use the Waterworks road to dwelling 35. The path passes between fences west and south of the dwelling. The mid-field continuation has been diverted south. Turn along the track to the black barn of Fulchers Farm, and resume the eastern progress here. A ditch on the right-hand side steers the diversion to a footbridge at the field junction.

Now back on the right-of-way follow the right-hand ditch out to Heron Hall drive. Ignore the path ahead and use the drive southwards to the telephone kiosk by 54 Billericay Road. A sidewalk extends left as far as 88 and the grass verge serves as a continuation to The Olde Dog Inn. Boots off first before entering the pub please.

Pub Yarns

Tilbury Hope was the scene of a battle in 1667 when a Dutch naval force reached the Thames bend. East Tilbury's St Catherine's church was damaged.

Some golf course contractors ignore the existence of footpaths and leave the new golfing patrons to sort out ensuing pedestrian traffic. Others plan around the footpaths, to offer mutual satisfaction to both sets of users.

East Horndon church, by the Country Park, is a red-brick gem with corner turrets and a stepped parapet.

Walk 9: Great Holland's Lions' Den

A walk along Tendring's sunshine coast provides a contrast to other walks in this chapter because it is beside a coast of attrition, and not by mudflats. Here a strand of glorious golden sand stretches 13 miles from The Naze to Colne Point. Great Holland enjoys a particularly nice section of this beach by Frinton-on-Sea, and it is shared with visitors on this Walk.

How to get there

Leave the A12 trunk road at the Ardleigh interchange for the A120 east and look for the water tower at Horsley Cross. Go south at the nearby roundabout on the B1035 to Thorpe le Soken. Merge with the B1033 and continue to Kirby Cross roundabout where another turn southwards uses the B1032 to Great Holland and The Lions' Den, map reference 169TM211191.

Buses	Clacton to Walton services 8, 9 & 10
Trains	Nearest station Kirby Cross with above bus connections

What is there?

Bungalows are in abundance around the two triangular road plans off the B1032 in Great Holland. Poking above the low rooflines are the tower of All Saints' church and the patina green turret of the non-conformist church.

The Lions' Den is to the south of these at an open junction with Little Clacton Road to the Nature Reserve.

This is a holiday area and the pub caters well for the 'passing trade', offering Ruddles ales, snacks, restaurant meals, children's room and meeting room. It has an ample car-park, but vehicles should not be left there without the landlord's permission. Alternative parking is at the Holland Haven Country Park where the B1032 joins the coastline.

Walk details

Walking distance	9 kms (5.6 miles) needing 135 minutes to stroll
Ordnance Survey maps	Landranger 169 Ipswich & The Naze. Pathfinder 1101 Clacton-on-Sea
Paths used	Great Holland 2, 3, 29, 5, 6, 38, 10.
District Council	Tendring

The Walk

From the Lions' Den walk along Main Road NE and fork right on to Manor Road, forking right again at The Ship to pass All Saints' church and join the footpath network off Church Lane. The middle of three paths emanating from Great Holland Hall is required. Fork right by the pond on to a concrete track and ignore Short Lane, signed as a public

GREAT HOLLAND

midfield paths

Mill

Nature Reserve

B1032

Manor Road

Little Clacton Road

The Lions Den

B1032 **START**

Long Lane

Dairyhouse Farm

FRINTON ON SEA

headland

Golf

Ⓚ B1032

Kirby Brook

greensward footway

Sandy Point

Holland Brook Pickers Ditch

Chevaux de Frise Point

RTG 142

NORTH SEA

Country Park

Ⓙ

HOLLAND HAVEN

WALKING DISTANCE 9kms

⑨

Schematic map; not to scale

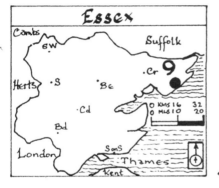

The Lions' Den
Little Clacton Road

Great Holland

CO13 OET

☎ 0255
675137

Day	Snacks		Meals	
	Ln	Eg	Ln	Eg
Sn	✔		✔	✔
M	✔	✔	✔	✔
T	✔	✔	✔	✔
W	✔	✔	✔	✔
Th	✔	✔	✔	✔
F	✔	✔	✔	✔
St	✔	✔	✔	✔

Walk Profile

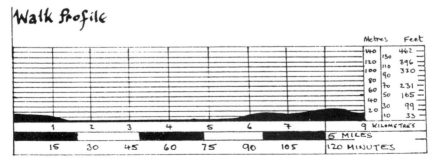

footpath. Stay on the harder track which has several·angular bends in its slow descent to the borrow dyke level by Frinton's golf course.

Beach

Long Lane is clearly marked across the fairways to the sea-wall. Mount the steps and decide whether to use the upper path or to walk on the smooth sands of the beach. Escape points are scarce, so do not race an incoming tide; use the beach only if it is broadly free of waves and likely to remain so for thirty minutes.

Sluices at the Holland Brook outfall plant block the beach route and a ramp enables the walltop path to be re-joined. Enter Holland Haven Country Park **(J.214169)** and use its vehicular exit to join the B1032. Turn right on the greensward and cross the bridges of Pickers Ditch and Holland Brook and look for the footpath sign off the second right-hand bend of the road **(K.210179)**.

Old Windmill

A farm headland begins westward from this layby and shortly swings right towards Dairyhouse Farm. The track is approximately co-linear with the line on the Pathfinder map, and the exit on to Little Clacton Road by the farmhouse.

Face the traffic coming from Great Holland and turn left on the lane to the east of the Holland Nature Reserve. Fork right by the base of the former smock mill and use the stile to go right with hedge on right. Continue NE from the hedge corner on a good mid-field path to a crossings of paths. Head SE to the hedge corner and continue through to Little Clacton Road again. Turn left to return to The Lions' Den just a few cottage garden widths away. Please replace or cover muddy footwear before going indoors.

Pub Yarns

A Rector of All Saints, Great Holland, already curate of Frinton and Little Clacton, had to re-build the church for his own Induction Service in the early 1700s.

Holland Haven was a small harbour where Holland Brook joined the sea. It silted up and a sluice system was installed to drain the brook. The silting probably curtailed the lucrative smuggling trade of the time.

Gun emplacements have been sited here from Napoleonic to modern times. A subsidiary defence strategy was to flood the marshes to impede the invader.

Today Holland Haven Country Park is a super habitat for preserving our diminishing stock of aquatic insect life.

Walk 10: Cold Norton's Norton Barge

The good clays of Essex make a rounded topography around Cold Norton and a few neighbouring parishes. These hillocks on the north side of the River Crouch are sometimes described as 'drumlinesque countryside'. Walking in this part of the county certainly dispels any notion that Essex is flat and monotonous. When wet, the clays of Essex can be both slippery and adhesive, and wellies with a good tread pattern can be the best footwear to combat the clay.

How to Get There

From the M25 Junction 29 take the A127 eastwards to the Wickford interchange with the A132. Proceed NE through Wickford to South Woodham Ferrers, and link with the B1012 road to Cold Norton. The Norton Barge is to the eastern side of the parish by a road narrowing bridge over the old railway line, map reference 168TL848004.

Buses	Maldon - Burnham 93B route
	Bradwell - South Woodham Ferrers routes 1 & 2
Trains	South Woodham Ferrers station on the Southminster branch line.

What is there?

A water tower by the crossroads and apparent ribbon development from there to the old railway bridge gives an initial forlorn impression, soon dispelled by exploration on foot.

The Norton Barge is one of those pubs to have added a restaurant to its licensed trade activity. Adnams, Courage and Greene King ales are sold. There is a garden plus parking spaces for patrons, but vehicles should not be left there without permission. Alternative parking can be found by the Howe Green Lane telephone kiosk near the crossroads.

Walk details

Walking distance	8 kms (5 miles) needing about 120 minutes to stroll
Ordnance Survey maps	Landranger 168 Colchester & The Blackwater
	Pathfinders 1123 Maldon, 1143 Burnham-on-Crouch
Paths used	Purleigh 14, 15, 31. Stow Maries 7, 11
	Cold Norton 20, 12, 13, 14, 8.
District Council	Maldon

The Walk

From the Norton Barge cross the narrow bridge where the B1012 crosses the former railway and turn right by the fencing of dwellings 56 & 58. Head SSE through to the southern end of the copse and see the beacon basket across the arable field by St Stephen's church. Adjust a little to the left to align with the reinstated path and climb it to cross St Stephen's Road by the churchyard.

The ensuing path has a crop growing on it, but an additional path skirts the NW corner of the field and joins the westward leading headland of the next field. At the junction of hedges (L.847996) turn right with hedge on right and then with the old railway cutting on the left, veer right to re-join St Stephen's Road.

Fairway

Cross the bridge left and ignore the road bend right in favour of the stile for footpath 13 off the outside of the bend. This path crosses the golf course and is waymarked with shin-high green and yellow markers so spaced as to allow the next one to be seen.

This excellent arrangement is almost co-linear with the right-of-way and informs golfers and walkers alike of what is going on. It leads to better harmony between two sets of recreational interests, which might not otherwise maintain.

Stow Maries

The waymarks continue WSW from the path junction and the exit is on Honey Pot Lane. Now in Stow Maries, go south and look for the waymark by a gap in the right-hand hedge. A grassy strip crosses the arable field to join Church Lane opposite the Old Rectory. Pass the church of St Mary & St Margaret to carefully cross the B1012 and enter path 7 which is the drive between Twin Chimneys and Sanditon.

Garden fences steer the path over a series of stiles in to the eastern edge of a rising pasture. Climb to the top stile and re-enter Cold Norton (M.830001). Two mid-field paths proceed NNE as worn by footfalls over two large fields towards Little Whitmans. An improvised stile with sheathed barbs indicates the crossing in to Purleigh parish.

Farther Howe Green

Turn right to walk in the pasture with hedge on the right-hand side and share a stiled exit on to Hackmans Lane. Face the oncoming traffic when

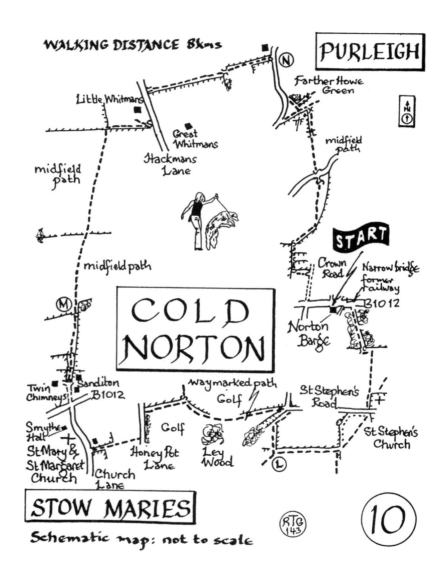

WALKING DISTANCE 8kms

PURLEIGH

Farther Howe Green

Little Whitmans

Great Whitmans

Hackmans Lane

midfield path

midfield path

midfield path

START

Crown Road

Narrow bridge former railway

B1012

Norton Barge

COLD NORTON

(M)

Twin Chimneys

Sanditon B1012

waymarked path Golf

St Stephen's Road

St Stephen's Church

Smythe Hall

Golf

St Mary & St Margaret Church

Honey Pot Lane

Ley Wood

(L)

Church Lane

STOW MARIES

RTG 143

(10)

Schematic map: not to scale

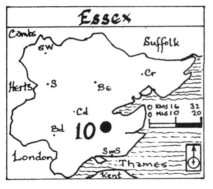

The Norton Barge
54 Latchingdon Road
Cold Norton
CM3 6JB

☎ 0621
      828253

Day	Snacks		Meals	
	L+E	£	L+E	£
Sn	✓	✓	✓	✓
M	✓	✓	✓	✓
T	✓	✓	✓	✓
W	✓	✓	✓	✓
Th	✓	✓	✓	✓
F	✓	✓	✓	✓
St	✓	✓	✓	✓

Walk Profile

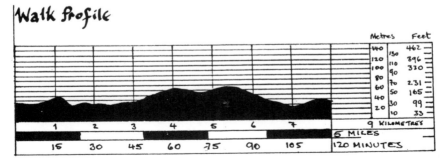

passing Little Whitmans and look for the bridge and waymark for path 15. Turn right to again have a hedge on the right-hand side to and beyond the crest of the hill. Swap sides of the hedge when over a double-planked bridge in a corner of hedges and descend to Howe Green Lane (N.838014). Turn right for Farther Howe Green.

Crown Road

Fork left along the edge of the Green to the bottom corner by a pole carrying overhead cables. Go left on the second path and immediately right over a bridge to follow the right-hand hedge SE to a cartbridge leading to the next field. The path continues through the arable crop up to a stile. Cross the hedged green lane and use the footbridge for access to the higher pasture.

Converge with the left-hand hedge to locate the stile in the SE corner. Now back in Cold Norton, cross three more stiles in a series of small paddocks before turning left along the northern edge of another plot of grazing and join unmade Crown Road. Turn right and then left along the sidewalk of Latchingdon Road, passing Clarke's Rise to return to The Norton Barge. Please remove muddy outdoor footwear before going indoors.

Pub Yarns

The former railway line was closed in 1953. It linked Maldon West to South Woodham Ferrers.

A holder of the living at St Stephen's when accused of dereliction of duty, pointed out that he only had a mud cottage to live in and it was difficult to perform his duties from there.

Recent repairs to Stow Maries church following wind damage suggests the area could have been suitable for a windmill. The water tower built in 1967 is on an exposed site. Windmills are no longer a common sight. They reached their peak of development at about the same time as clippers were at the zenith of wind power at sea. Just as boat sails were seen on the Crouch so postmill sails with their fantails were seen inland.

Walk 11: Burnham-on-Crouch's Star Inn

Burnham-on-Crouch is the largest settlement on the Dengie peninsula, it unites the agriculture of the region with the seafaring life of the broad seaways. The land of Dengie juts out between the Crouch and Blackwater, low and vulnerable to flooding, destined perhaps to join Dengie Flats, unless more Dutch-like defences against the encroaching seas are made. Since the creation of the Woolwich Barrage on the Thames, the town sea-wall at Burnham has been reinforced and it doubles as a fine promenade.

How to get there

Leave the A12 trunk road at the A414 interchange on Chelmsford bypass and select the B1010 from the Oak roundabout at Woodham Mortimer. The B1010 leads to Burnham-on-Crouch where it merges with the B1021 to cross the railway bridge and enter the town centre. The Star Inn is on the right-hand side between the war memorial and the clock tower, map reference 168TQ951956.

Buses	Routes 4, 5, 96, 98, 99 (and 631 on summer Sundays) terminate at Burnham. Some connect with Bradwell-on-Sea and South Woodham Ferrers and most with Maldon via villages of the Dengie peninsula.
Trains	Burnham is the penultimate station on the Southminster branch line.

What is there?

Burnham-on-Crouch is a busy small town which enjoys its waterfront and concentrates most of its action around The Royal Corinthian Yacht Club, the Clock tower and other yacht and sailing clubs. Pubs, shops and a museum are to be found by the High Street cul de sac. Mangapps Railway Museum, St Mary's church and the railway station are to be found along the approach roads to Burnham. Burnham Week and Burnham Carnival are the highlights of each active summer, and in 1993 Burnham-on-Crouch successfully hosted The East Coast Boat Show. The Star Inn provides sustenance, including Ridleys ales. The restaurant and bar are augmented by a paved garden off the promenade. It is finely situated so that it fronts both the High Street and the seafront. Parking is in High Street with the overflow by the library and sports centre between The Star and the station.

Walk details

Walking distance	8.6 kms (5.4 miles) needing about 130 minutes to stroll
Ordnance Survey maps	Landranger 168 Colchester & The Blackwater
	Pathfinder 1143 Burnham-on-Crouch
Paths used	Burnham 11, 21, 22, 17, 18, 15, 5.
District Council	Maldon

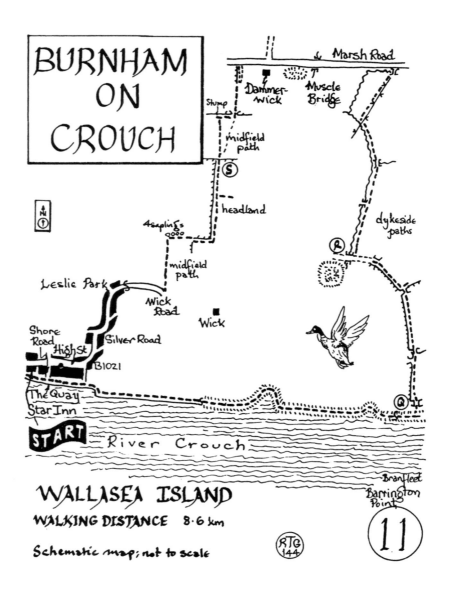

BURNHAM ON CROUCH

Marsh Road

Dammer-wick

Muscle Bridge

Stump

midfield path

(S)

headland

4 saplings

dykeside paths

(R)

midfield path

Leslie Park

Wick Road

Wick

Shore Road

High St

Silver Road

B1021

The Quay

Star Inn

(Q)

START

River Crouch

Branfleet
Barrington Point

WALLASEA ISLAND

WALKING DISTANCE   8·6 km

Schematic map; not to scale

RTG 144

11

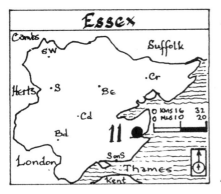

The Star Inn

29 High Street

Burnham-on-Crouch

CMO 8AG

☎ 0621
       782010

Day	Snacks		Meals	
	Lu	Eg	Lu	Eg
Sn	✓	✓	✓	✓
M	✓	✓	✓	✓
T	✓		✓	
W	✓	✓	✓	✓
Th	✓	✓	✓	✓
F	✓	✓	✓	✓
St	✓	✓	✓	✓

Walk Profile

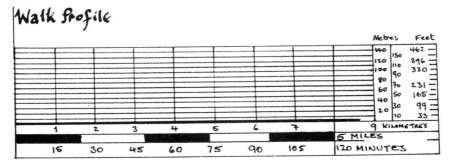

The Walk

Leave The Star via the courtyard and turn left on the red promenade walk along the glorious front passing the moorings and proceeding eastwards beyond the floodgates on an earthen wall. It is a thirty minute stroll along this wall from the tiered windows of The Royal Corinthian Yacht Clubhouse to Branfleet Spit formed where the River Roach unites with the Crouch.

Barrington Point on Wallasea Island is more exactly opposite the bridge over the borrow dyke waymarked as path 17 **(Q.980953)**. Turn inland here to a series of paths rounding Dammerwick which is in view from the wall. The headland skirts a dyke before bending by a copse. Cross a bridge by the bend to use a lesser path still beside a dyke until another bridge connects with the track from Redward to Burnham Wick.

Go westwards to the double waymarked bridge and along the concrete track to tree-lined Pannels Brook where reservoir banking marks the spot **(R.972960)** for a three-way signpost. Turn right to walk the eastern bank of the brook, passing a sluice and cross a field-dividing ditch by footbridge to round Pannel's curve until under a set of power lines.

Muscle Bridge

Path eighteen uses the nearest available cultivation line, in the absence of a reinstated path, under the line of these pole-carried wires out to a bridged exit on Marsh Road. A subsidiary brook is roughly parallel with this line, but no permissive path could be found beside it.

Head westwards along Marsh Road, using Muscle Bridge to cross Pannel's Brook. Pass the front of Dammerwick and turn left by the cypress hedge of the steading's western border. A concrete drive becomes a headland leading southward to join an east-west headland. Look SSW for the reinstated path to a hedged field junction **(S.961964)**. It may be necessary to go 1.5 minutes (100 metres) along the headland to search for a cultivation line from the fourth stump, if there is no reinstatement.

Burnham Wick

Pass through the gap in the hedge and walk the new headland with young trees on the right-hand side, passing the headland junction left, and locating the right turn of path 15 by the grazing hedge corner.

A hedge and a fence steer the path westward out beyond the grazing, across a joining of arable fields to a stand of four young trees. Here the path clearly bends southward to join Wick Road.

Go acutely right to use Wick Road as a route in to Burnham town. Ignore turnings in to Leslie Park, Ramblers Way and Orchard Road and use Silver Road to find the eastern end of High Street. Enjoy the charm of High Street's facades back to The Star Inn. Please remove outdoor muddy footwear before entering the inn.

Pub Yarns

Hundreds of people were employed during the 19th century alongside the Crouch in the fishing industry of which oyster fishing was dominant. At a court case before Witham magistrates in 1894 it was estimated that the value of oyster culture was a quarter of a million pounds sterling. Conservation of oyster stocks is regulated to this day.

Yachting began to replace commercial shipping in the 1900s. The construction of the railway link to London via Wickford helped Burnham survive the decline of oyster fishing.

During Burnham week as many as 400 craft in a score of different sizes and shapes, and all energetically crewed, maybe seen in pursuit of trophies in the country's biggest regatta after Cowes. Ocean-going boats race out to the Barrow Deep buoy and back.

A ferry service operating mainly at weekends to Wallasea Island has recently resumed in response to the demand of tourism.

Walk 12: Brightlingsea's Brewers' Arms

Brightlingsea is as bright and breezy as its name suggests. The light over Hurst Green often draws comment, and this walk heads straight there to savour the great estuary, peaceful when compared with commercial activity around the fame of Aldous shipbuilding last century.

The walk continues around Flag Creek which probably once, and may yet again, cause Brightlingsea to be an island. Seafaring is very much part of its heritage and Brightlingsea is a Cinque Port.

How to get there

Brightlingsea is at the southern terminus of the B1029 road which can be joined off the A12 trunk road by the Stratford St Mary-Dedham underpass. Follow the road in to Brightlingsea, passing the East Anglian style perpendicular church tower and the secondary school.

Notice the Cherry Tree pub and fork left soon afterwards to use Ladysmith Avenue's approach to Victoria Place, the hub of the landlubbers' part of Brightlingsea. The Brewers' Arms is opposite St James' Church and its car-park is in New Street, map reference 169TM087167. Alternative parking is along High Street nearer the Hurst Green end.

Buses	Services 78, 74, 178 and 127 connect with Colchester and with Clacton-on-Sea
Trains	Great Bentley station via 127 buses

What is there?

A colourful open space is the attractive central feature of this small town. The main church is passed on the approach road and the functional church of St James' is at the Victoria Place end of High Street. Midway along High Street is Jacobes, a building notable for some fourteenth century features. The Brewers' Arms has a warm and welcoming appearance, like a street-side cafe brought over from Europe with flower-strewn tables at the front. Behind there is good beer and a function room.

Walk details

Distance	8 kilometres (5 miles) needing about two hours to stroll
Ordnance Survey sheets	Landranger 168 Colchester & The Blackwater 169 Ipswich & The Naze
	Pathfinder 1100 Bradwell & Mersea Island. Fringe 1101
Paths used	Brightlingsea 12, 31, 13, 25, 24, 8, 27, 5, 7. Thorrington 17, 14, 8.
District Council	Tendring

The Walk

From the Brewers' Arms walk the length of High Street to Hurst Green and turn right by dwelling 102 to descend Backwaterside Lane to the marshland level at the corner of the left-hand field. Walk left by a grassy path by a reed-filled ditch to the corner of the right-hand compound of grazing plots. Turn right and cross the sleeper bridge to gain the top sea-wall path.

Oyster Beds

Get left of the shipyard fencing to have open views across Brightlingsea Creek and the two parts of Cindery Island. Over St Osyth Point is Brightlingsea Reach. At low tide the oyster layings are visible.

A boatyard on the sea-wall forces the path inland on to Rope Walk, a straight causeway across the marshland. Where the track bends left to join Mill Street, go right instead on to an earthen sea-wall above the honeycomb of old oyster pits some dating back 300 years.

Follow the wall left around the terminus of high cables to approach some gardens, one of which has a fence extending across the borrow dyke to give an appearance of a penal institution. Carefully skirt this fencing to a niche (V.097166) in the sea-wall where barges probably once swapped cargoes of manure for hay to trade in London's docks.

Pitscape

Ignore the path out to the channel. Go inland instead between fences to emerge opposite an attractive pond. Walk right along Mill Street to rustically elegant East End Green and bear left on to Robinson Road which is followed as far as Granville Way.

Walk on the path opposite Granville Way, going right on the stones of Stoney Lane. Reap the scenic benefit of yesteryear's policy of reforming old extraction pits in to pitscapes of infinite interest. Bear left of the silver fir tree at Marsh Farmhouse and follow the copper beech hedge to the paddock.

A stile admits the path to a strip of land by the eastern hedge and a matching stile allows continuance of the NE descent to a track at marshland level. Go right over the stiled gateway and mount the

THORRINGTON

BRIGHTLINGSEA

marshland grazing path

Crocky Grove byre

marshland grazing path

Morses Farm

mid pasture path

wall top path

Flag Creek

Campernell Close

Red Barn Road

Stoney Lane

Marsh Farm

105

Regent Road

pitscape

Granville Way

East End Green

Robinson Road

Queen Street

Victoria Place

St James' Church

HURST GREEN

East End Farm

Mill St

Brewers' Arms

Jacobes

Back Waterside Lane

High Street

Seawall path

Shipyard

Boatyard

Rope Walk

START

WALKING DISTANCE 8km

Schematic Map: not to scale

RTG 145

(12)

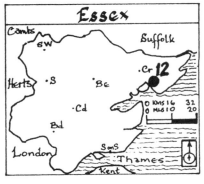

The Brewers' Arms
1 Victoria Place
Brightlingsea
CO7 0BX

☎ 0206
302028

Day	Snacks		Meals	
	Ln	Eg	Ln	Eg
Sn	✓			
M	✓			
T	✓			
W	✓			
Th	✓			
F	✓			
St	✓			

Walk Profile

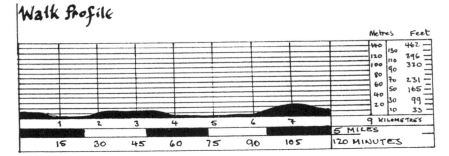

Thorrington sea-wall.

Marshland Byre

Walk the Flag Creek path atop the western wall and go round with it to continue eastwards as far as the bend SE to face the distant caravans below Hollybush Hill. Leave the sea-wall at this bend (**W.102182**) and bridge the borrow dyke to surmount the sheathed electric fence stile and enter the eastern side of a marshland pasture. Head for the a stand of half a dozen oak trees in the NE corner and bear left along the raised track to the exit stile by the trough.

A fenced path ensues linking westward with a track down from Thorrington Wood. The track ends at the lonely byre and the path continues westward between hedges to a stiled entrance to pasture south of Crocky Grove. Pass the trees to go under the wires and by the trough and bear left at an old tree stock. Heading WSW, and just left of the church tower, cross the stile on to the next pasture and find two footbridges in series across mid-field rills to the exit stile and footbridge.

Cinque Port Town

Chamfer the SE corner of the arable field to find a cradle bridge (**X.088185**) back in to Brightlingsea. Cross SSE to the pasture and the high exit stile to Morses Lane. Climb the lane and pass the farmhouse and most of the buildings looking for a stile and waymark pointing left.

Enter the grazing and head southwards, with wood on left, pass a right-hand convex corner of an industrial estate and converge with overhead wires by the exit stile near the housing of Campernell Close. Fencing steers the path out to 105 Red Barn Road.

Turn left and right on to Regent Road. The sidewalk links with Queen Street and leads back to Victoria Place. Around to the left is St James' church and opposite is The Brewers' Arms at the top of New Street. Muddy outdoor boots should be replaced or covered before going indoors.

Pub Yarns

The hundred foot tower of All Saints Church, and Bateman's tower, and important landmarks for boats in the estuary. The church is now open only in the summer. St.James' church in the town centre by the Brewers' Arms acts as the parish church.

Brightlingsea is the Saxon settlement of Beorhtrics island.

People of Brightlingsea know too well the peril of the sea. In March 1883 three smacks and a barge were lost in a gale at sea with the loss of all hands. Thirty-two children were left fatherless. In All Saints church two hundred and six tiles commemorate sailors lost since 1872.

Apart from fishing, merchant seamanship and yachting, Brightlingsea, as well as Burnham, Tollesbury, Manningtree and Mistley, Mersea and Maldon, has provided formidable crew members for the fighting Navy at battles from the Crecy campaign, through the Armada and Napoleonic conflicts, to the two World Wars.

The railway arrived in 1861. People like the Rev Sabine Baring-Gould could travel across from Mersea on the ferry to use the train to London. The timber swing bridge over Alresford Creek always looked fragile under the weight of steam engines.

Regent Road, like other roads in our environment, was a fieldpath before it was a residential road.

Section Two:
Rambles by
The County Borders

Essex, as the kingdom of the East Saxons, and later as a region or county
has been in existence for hundreds of years. People living there now
identify with Essex County Council, to whom they pay some rates and
taxes, and which has been in its local government place for the last one
hundred years. Along the non-coastal boundaries of Essex are other
counties where the neighbouring treatments of things like highways are
readily inspected.

BOUNDARY FORCES

Why are the boundaries where they are? What forces, disputes or
compromises established the northern and western boundaries in such a
way that they have endured for so long? Will the national government
chip a bit more of Essex away to form another London Borough, as
happened at Redbridge, Havering and Waltham Forest to name but a
few areas lost in the sixties?

CURIOSITY

Questions like these recur as walks are made in the vicinity of the
counties bordering Essex. Kent, for so long separated from Essex by
unbridgeable water, is now linked by the M25 Queen Elizabeth II Bridge.
Walks overlooking Kent have been included in Chapter One as Thames
estuary walks. Against Hertfordshire, Cambridgeshire and Suffolk bor-
ders, the sense of territorial loyalty is strong. Proposals for marginal
border changes are resisted.

FORESTS

Two of the eight walks in this chapter are close to London and both
utilise remnants of ancient forests, once part of the Forest of Essex. Both

Epping and Hainault Forests are hard against the urban fringe of the Capital where they are successfully managed to provide many forms of recreation for their related populations, as well as to add a seasoning of foliage to the scenery and a habitat for brave wildlife.

Broadleaved trees such as lime, oak, beech, hornbeam, hazel, birch, ash and chestnut may be seen, with a little evidence of former elm glory too. Coppiced trees and pollarded trees are in evidence. The coppicing method of woodland management, based roughly upon a twenty year cycle, is followed by conservationists in parts of the forests today.

WALKS

The highest point in Essex is by the Cambridgeshire border. Walk 17 passes nearby without actually visiting the site, because there is nothing of note there. Higher land is visible in nearby Hertfordshire and Cambridgeshire. Nevertheless it is an extremely interesting walk, and it shares a path with The Icknield Way, one of the most ancient of Britain's highways.

Constable Country is in Essex too, the only region named after a painter. Walk 14 is by Dedham Vale and two other walks share the beautiful Stourdale scenery with Suffolk.

All public footpaths should be a metre wide and fieldside paths wider.

Walk 13: Steeple Bumpstead's Fox & Hounds

Steeple Bumpstead is located where two B class roads bridge Bumpstead Brook. This stream eagerly flows off the East Anglian heights around Helions Bumpstead and the Cambridgeshire Camps to scour a valley towards its confluence with the River Stour at Wixoe on the Suffolk border. Within a mile, as the Walk reveals, are the headwaters of the River Colne. Despite the proximity, the height difference rules out river capture.

How to get there

Leave the A604 main road for the B1054 by the Little Chef at Birdbrook. At Claywall Bridge in Steeple Bumpstead bear left on to the B1057 Chapel Street towards Finchingfield. The Fox & Hounds, map reference 154TL680410, is at the corner of Church Street and Chapel Street by the timbered Moot Hall which forms a traffic island.

Buses	Saffron Walden - Haverhill services 8, 23, 38, 19.
Trains	Nearest stations at Sudbury and Wendens Ambo (Audley End) are too far away to be viable.

What is there?

Steeple Bumpstead seems a most agreeable community with evidence of church involvement in school development last century, and of Braintree District Council's current schemes to keep the rural community alive. A modern Village Hall is under construction in 1993. The ford is a fine feature which can be by-passed when necessary by using Claywall Bridge. The church dates from the eleventh century and is a large building for that period. Local walkers have improved the parish footpath network. The Fox & Hounds is an attractive small pub anxious to please customers. It has a restaurant area and facilities for disabled customers. Greene King and Ind Coope ales are served. Car parking is limited. An alternative is in Bowerhall Drive.

Walk details

Walking distance	8 kms (5 miles) requiring 120 minutes to stroll
Ordnance Survey maps	Landranger 154 Cambridge & Newmarket
	Pathfinder 1028 Haverhill and Clare
Paths used	Steeple Bumpstead 10, 15, 12, 20, 23, 22, 18, 39.
	Birdbrook 13, 14, 15.
District Council	Braintree

The Walk

Thread through the snicket north side of The Fox & Hounds towards the old National school-building. Go down Church Street sidewalk by the Red Lion and the Lockup and round the bend as far as The Crescent.

Pass the terrace fronting this footway and cross Bumpstead Brook bridge to turn right to walk brookside as far as Claywall Bridge.

Use sidewalks left and then right on Haverhill Road and where the B1057 bends left, continue straight on along The Endway as far as the signpost right for footpath 15. Use the reinstated line towards a foot-bridge over the brook. Stay north side of the water and walk brookside ENE for two fields and the connecting footbridge.

This is not quite the line given on the O.S. map, but compliance with a local diversion. From the corner of the second field the exit squeezes by a left-hand fence out to a lane with a ford to Broad Green. A footbridge bypasses the ford by a red mail box. Turn left to face oncoming B1054 traffic as far as Rylands.

Rise To Birdbrook

Path 20 is signposted by a transformer on stilts northside of the cypress hedge. Climb the fieldside path to Moyns Wood and use the vehicular tracks north and east of the woodland. Now in Birdbrook, head for the eastern boundary of the next field and turn left at the top on to a headland. This heads eastwards and leaves it where it bends by Church-field Grove.

Pass the northern side of the Grove and cross the small field SE to a waymark by the churchyard hedge. Enter the churchyard and pass the fine church of St Augustine's to join Moat Road in Birdbrook. To the right is The Plough, a thatched pub to match the thatched Community House SW along the sidewalk.

Moyns Park

Beyond the pond, turn right on to a tree-lined drive to Moyns Park. This is also a footpath offering a fine wooded habitat back in to the parish of Steeple Bumpstead.

Any rainwater sloping off left is destined to join the River Colne and may be seen later from Walks 28 and 12 of this book. Leave the lakes, moat, farm and Moyns Hall on the left-hand side by veering right until the drive bends left beyond the ha ha (Y.693407). A post and rail fence encloses a pasture on the right-hand side. Footpath 23 crosses it. Wriggle through the rails between trough and white gate, or divert to use the

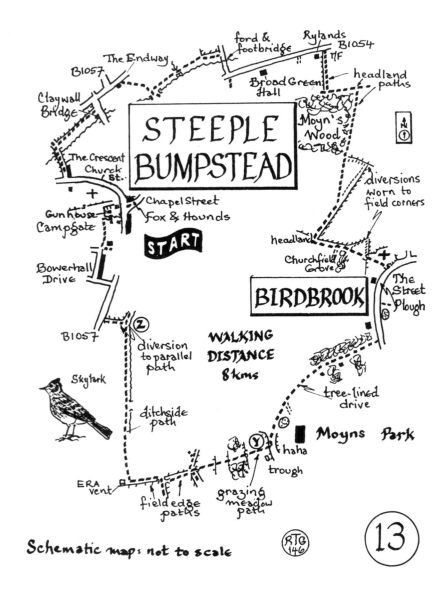

ford &
footbridge   Rylands
B1054
The Endway   T/F
B1057   Broad Green   headland
Hall   paths
Claywall   N↑
Bridge   Moyn's
Wood
The Crescent
Church   diversions
St.   worn to
field corners
Gun house Chapel Street
Camp Gate Fox & Hounds   headland
Churchfield
START   Grove   + L
Bowerhall   BIRDBROOK   The
Drive   Street
Plough
B1057   Z
diversion   WALKING
to parallel   DISTANCE
path   8 kms
Skylark   tree-lined
drive
ditchside
path   Moyns   Park

ERA   haha
vent   Y
trough
field edge   grazing
paths   meadow
path

STEEPLE
BUMPSTEAD

Schematic maps not to scale   RTG
146   ⑬

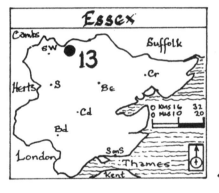

The Fox & Hounds

3 Chapel Street

Steeple Bumpstead

Essex

☎ 0440 730281

Day	Snacks		Meals	
	Ln	Eg	Ln	Eg
Sn	✓			
M	✓			
T	✓	✓		
W	✓	✓		
Th	✓	✓		
F	✓	✓		
St	✓	✓		

Walk Profile

Metres		Feet	
140	130	462	
120	110	396	
100	90	330	
80	70	231	
60	50	165	
40	30	99	
20	10	33	

1	2	3	4	5	6	7	9 KILOMETRES
							5 MILES
15	30	45	60	75	90	105	120 MINUTES

gate, and cross the grass westwards for the gate under the trees. The path follows a direct line through the clearing to merge with another path by its exit stile.

Stour Catchment

Turn left and head SW with hedge on right, cross the footbridge and immediately cross another slatted bridge to its right. Turn left again, this time with ditch on left-hand side for a few paces to an E R A venting station, where the downhill path through the field to Steeple Bumpstead is clearly etched.

Now back in the Stour catchment, descend to the convex hedge corner (Z.683409) and turn left on path 39 supplanting the mapped diagonal path 18 connecting with Finchingfield Road. Go downhill and enter Bowerhall Drive by the red mail box.

Swing right to enter the recreation ground by the new Village Hall and cross Campgate's greensward towards the church tower peeping above the horse-chestnut trees. Look right to see a cherry tree by a convex garden corner. Near it is a five-barred gate and a stile. Use it to have the dilapidated elegance of Gun House on the left-hand side. Pass along the drive by The Vicarage and cross the road with care from the war memorial to the Moot Hall and so return to the Fox & Hounds. Muddy outdoor footwear should be washed in the ford, removed, or covered before entering the pub, please.

Pub Yarns

Did you notice any references to Nurse Edith Cavell? She was shot by a German firing squad in Brussels for helping soldiers to escape to Britain in 1915. Her connection with Steeple Bumpstead is noted by a road nameplate on the Bowerhall estate, and more about her may be read in the church.

Moyns Park takes its name from the original fourteenth century owner Robert de FitzWilliam le Moigne. The le Moignes' dynasty prevailed for 200 years and after Joan le Moigne married William Gent of Suffolk in the sixteenth century, the Gents continued there for another 400 years, its occupants being very much involved with the War of the Roses and the Civil War. The building is H-shaped in plan, and was sited with defence in mind on the Colne-Stour watershed.

Walk 14: Little Horkesley's Beehive

The Area of Outstanding Natural Beauty designation associated with Constable Country has recently been extended to include Little Horkesley and Wormingford. The views across to the Suffolk side of the Stour valley are quite stunning. The Beehive is situated at the village centre of Little Horkesley near St Peter & St Paul's church which was destroyed by enemy bombing during World War II and rebuilt in 1958.

How to get there

Little Horkesley is between the Queen's Head on the B1508 road in Wormingford, and the Rose & Crown on the A134 road in Great Horkesley, both of which are accessible from the A12 slip road signed (A134) at Lexden near Colchester. From the A12 spur roundabout by Colchester Camping join the A604 east to link with A134. Go north under the railway bridge at North Station. Fork left on the B1508, proceed through West Bergholt and turn right in Wormingford by the triangular junction with a bus shelter. A country road extends eastward to form a crossroads at the Beehive, map reference 168TL961321.

Buses	Service 84A Colchester - Sudbury twice each way per week only. Other services to Bures along the B1508, by Chambers and by Beestons buses are more frequent and pass a short way off Wormingford church. Sundays 601 & 757 services.
Trains	Colchester North and use bus to Wormingford.

What is there?

Little Horkesley has a charming crossroad junction completed by a war memorial, bus shelter and The Beehive. The bus shelter keeps a map of the parish rights-of-way dry. Buses are very occasional. The Beehive has a restaurant with obliging staff, well used to serving walkers with Greene King ales and other drinks in this popular Constable Country walking area. A phoned booking for food is appreciated. There is a car-park for patrons. Alternative parking is along the verge of School Road or Lane.

Walk details

Walking distance	8 kms (5 miles) needing about 2 hours to stroll
Ordnance Survey maps	Landranger 168 Colchester & The Blackwater
	Pathfinder 1052 Halstead (north) & Nayland
Paths used	Little Horkesley 29, 7, 22, 8, 5 , 3.
	Wormingford 21,30, 32, 3, 2, 23, 25,
District Council	Colchester

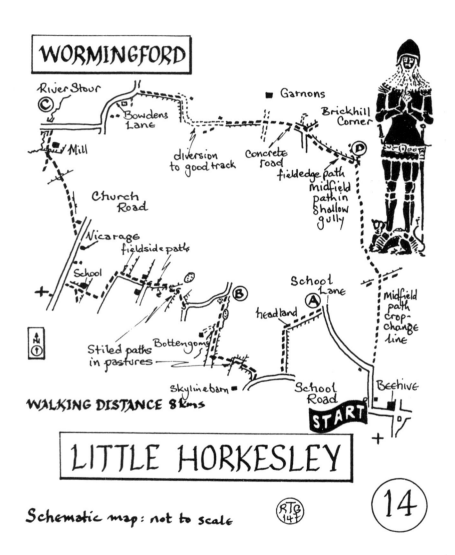

WORMINGFORD

River Stour

Bowdens Lane

Mill

diversion to good track

Garnons

Brickhill Corner

Concrete road

fieldedge path
midfield
path in
shallow
gully

Church Road

Vicarage
fieldside paths

School

School Lane

headland

Midfield path crop-change line

Stiled paths in pastures

Bottengoms

WALKING DISTANCE 8 kms

Skyline barn

School Road

Beehive

START

LITTLE HORKESLEY

Schematic map: not to scale

14

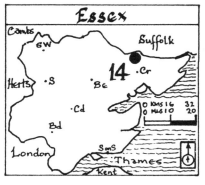

The Beehive
School Road
Little Horkesley
CO6 4DH

please
phone

☎ **0206**
271610

Day	Snacks		Meals	
	Ln	Eg	Ln	Eg
Sn	✓	✓	✓	✓
M	✓	✓	✓	✓
T	✓	✓	✓	✓
W	✓	✓	✓	✓
Th	✓	✓	✓	✓
F	✓	✓	✓	✓
St	✓	✓	✓	✓

Walk Profile

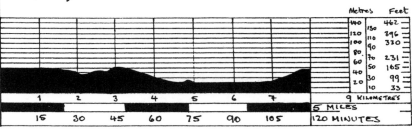

The Walk

Move westwards from The Beehive along School Road and turn right on to School Lane. Bend left with the tarmac of the lane and begin the descent in to the verdant valley of the languid River Stour.

A third of the way down the hillside, where signposts indicate a path crossing (**A.956324**), turn on to the left-hand grassy headland, and enjoy the views across the valley as the westward direction is resumed.

At the end of the bank, turn left again, to a narrower grassy track following the left-hand hedge as far as the steps down to a country lane. Turn right and face any oncoming traffic for 140 metres before re-entering the same field, this time via a footbridge. Keep the high hedge on the left-hand side and go through the gap under the twin-poled support for overhead wires.

Bottengoms Stream

Maintain the westerly direction, now with a fence on the right-hand side, and enter the next grazing plot via the corner stile. Converge with the overhead wires to locate the matching exit stile at the foot of the slope. Follow the hedgeline downstream to its confluence with Bottengoms stream and cross the bridge to be west side of the pond. Continue by the plantation of young trees to join Garnons Chase (**B.947323**).

Use this country lane to go uphill left and leave it where it dips to swing left. A stile on the outer bend indicates the path across the next stream tumbling down to join the Stour. Follow the right-hand hedge through the grazing and continue off the convex corner descending to a point between the trough and the pond. Here locate a double stiled footbridge. Cross the narrow grazing plot to the matching double stile footbridge marking the exit just below a cluster of four oak trees. In the third grazing field rise with the fence line left towards the flint walls of Folly Cottage.

Flint School

Exit via a kissing gate and cross the end of Colletts Chase to pass Folly Cottage. Ignore the matching kissing gate, using instead the stile beside the fieldgate. A headland ensues westward with hedge on the left-hand side and glorious views usually available to the right.

Swing around the hedge corner left and swing right to follow the change-crop line out to the flint walls of Wormingford School. Pass through the gate and share the school drive out to the road.

The church of St.Andrews is worth seeing before continuing with the route northwards along Church Road until just beyond the Rectory. A signpost points out a mid-field path following under the wires towards Wormingford Mill.

Wormingford Mill

Descend the ever-steepening slope in the valley, over the stile to merge with another path using the same stile in to the Mill garden. Cross to the white railings by the old mill race and share the drive out to the signpost beside Wormingford bridge spanning the Stour from Essex in to Suffolk. **(C.933329)**.

Stay Essex side to climb Mill Hill and select Bowdens Lane going left from the T-junction. Ignore the first two signposts for footpaths right, and take the third, a concrete bridleway heading back towards Little Horkesley.

Garnon Country

The concrete does not exactly follow the right-of-way, but is pretty well co-linear with it and is regularly used in preference for going mid-crop. A section of gravelled track connects a break in the concrete surface, which continues across the end of Garnons Chase and joins the bottom of School Lane by the site of the former Brickhill Cottages.

Two signposts point left off the tarmac lane. Select the upper one and walk beside the bank as far as the footbridge **(D.958327)** of a cross-path down the valley side. Turn uphill on to this path following the curving line of a contoured cleavage in mid-field heading for a gap in the upper hedgeline. From the gap the path continues by a pole and an oak tree along a change variety cropping line out to the bend of School Lane walked earlier. Continue southwards and turn left on to School Road to return to The Beehive. Please remove any mud from footwear before entering the pub.

Pub Yarns

Richard Fitz Godebold founded a Priory for Cluniac Monks at Little Horkesley. The Priory, a sixteenth century house, is on the site today.

From about the same time we get Josselyns and a century later Lower Dairy House. Both are just off the walking route but may be seen from a car on the road to Nayland.

Wormingford was a Saxon ford controlled by Withemund.

A creature from the nearby mere was slain by Sir George de la Haye in medieval times. Some like to associate this story with the legend of St George and the Dragon. The scene is depicted in a church window commemorating the war efforts of those stationed at Wormingford airfield.

Painter John Nash lived here until 1977 and writer Ronald Blythe still enthuses for the area.

Walk 15: High Beach's King's Oak

This part of Epping Forest, is it High Beach or is it spelt High Beech? Some of the soil on the ridge between the rivers Roding and Lee (or Lea!) may be heath-like but there surely is not enough sandiness to make a beach. Yet beech trees are bountiful and beautiful in this forest, one of the higher places in Essex - 117 metres compared with Danbury at 107 metres A O D - so high beeches they are. Signposts read High Beach and Holy Innocents church declares itself to be at High Beach, so High Beach will suffice. Nearby is the border with the London Borough of Waltham Forest and over the river Lee is both current Hertfordshire and the former Middlesex. A recent man-made feature in the forest is the hoggin dressed bridleway, orange in colour and broad in width, which makes navigation relatively simple. This Walk uses a linkage of these bridleways as a route-skeleton. The idea is to walk off them, using them as intermittent - say once or twice per three minutes - visual handrails. It takes confidence, but you do not carry on rewardless.

How to get there

Leave the M25 at junction 26 and use the A 121 towards Loughton as far as the City Limits roundabout where the A104 south is connected. At the next roundabout, by the Robin Hood, turn right and within a furlong veer right from Fairmead Road and then fork right from the tree-surrounded church to find The King's Oak on the right-hand side of Wake Road just before the next road junction, map reference 177TQ412982.

The Epping Forest Conservation Centre is just east of the King's Oak and there are ample direction signs pointing the route to this field studies centre.

Trains	Nearest station Loughton and connect by taxi to High Beach or bus to Goldings Hill map reference 428985.
Buses	Routes 201 and 502 Loughton to Epping pass the Walk at Goldings Hill, as do routes 8 and 250 Loughton towards Waltham Cross.

What is there?

The three-storeyed King's Oak dominates an open space in a broadleaf forest. Waltham Abbey and other settlements in and beyond the Lee valley are on view from Rushey Plain. There are conveniences and a field studies centre near the pub. Also nearby is a kerbed hard-surface path designed for wheelchairs to enter the forest. The King's Oak is geared to cope with heavy demand by offering garden, restaurant, meeting room and serving Burtons beers and M & B ales. There is live music for weekend discos. Parking is liberal, with alternative places at most road crossings along this Walk.

Walk details

Walking distance	8.6 kms (5.4 miles) needing 130 minutes to stroll
Ordnance Survey maps	Landranger 177 East London,167 Chelmsford & Harlow. Pathfinder 1141 Loughton & Harold Hill with a few metres on 1121 Epping and Chipping Ongar.
Paths used	All within the confines of the Epping Forest Act of 1882.
District Council	Epping Forest

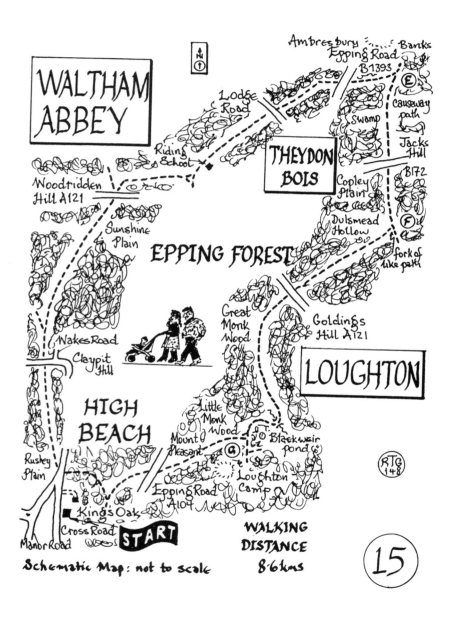

WALTHAM ABBEY

Ambresbury — Banks
Epping Road B1393
E
Lodge Road
Swamp
Causeway path
Jacks Hill
THEYDON BOIS
Copley Plain
B172
Riding School
Woodridden Hill A121
Sunshine Plain
Dulsmead Hollow
F
EPPING FOREST
fork of like path
Great Monk Wood
Goldings Hill A121
Wakes Road
Claypit Hill
LOUGHTON
HIGH BEACH
Little Monk Wood
Mount Pleasant
Blackweir pond
G
Rushey Plain
Loughton Camp
RTG 148
Epping Road A104
King's Oak
Cross Road
START
Manor Road

Schematic Map: not to scale

WALKING DISTANCE
8.6 kms

15

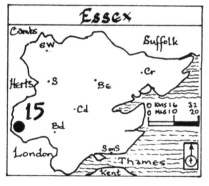

The King's Oak
Wake Road
High Beach
Essex.

☎ 081
5085000

Day	Snacks		Meals	
	Ln	Es	Ln	Es
Sn	✓	✓	✓	✓
M	✓	✓	✓	✓
T	✓	✓	✓	✓
W	✓	✓	✓	✓
Th	✓	✓	✓	✓
F	✓	✓	✓	✓
St	✓	✓	✓	✓

Walk Profile

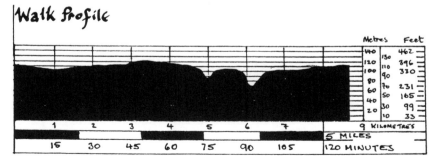

The Walk

From the King's Oak turn right along Wake Road and merge with Manor Road. The three-way road junction is augmented by two openings on to bridleways. Cross to the layby which usually houses a forest green hut selling teas and snacks and turn right to select the bridleway heading NE parallel with the road. A waymark declares this to be part of a long distance route to Hatfield Forest. The track diverges from the road sufficiently to be parted from it by a forest screen.

Honey Lane Quarters

Claypit Hill is the first road to be crossed. The bridleway duly continues over the road. Soon fork right NE to diverge slightly from any traffic noise on an out-of-sight Wake Road in a part of the forest known as Honey Lane Quarters. Some wood-chippings are used to surface part of the bridleway in an experiment which hopefully will prove successful because wood chippings belong to the forest. Garish orange hoggin looks alien, even when sullied with mud.

Woodridden Hill presents busy A121 traffic to cross. The nearby City Limits roundabout slows approach vehicles down but those leaving the junction can accelerate alarmingly in eagerness to get to the M25. Cross carefully and again fork right to be parallel with the road just crossed and then bear NE left to keep the riding school on the right-hand side.

Lodge Road has less frequent traffic. Again cross carefully to continue NE to a crossing of Epping Road, the B1393 which also requires much head twisting and two-way assessments of vehicular speeds before a successful crossing is made.

Long Running

Floor vegetation changes to plants suitable for the swampy habitat of Long Running just south of Ambresbury Banks. Any off-bridleway navigation is best done north side, to visit the ancient earthworks. The bridleway takes a clear passage to a junction with a like track.(**E.436002**) Turn right to use a raised path through Long Running to the car parking space by Jacks Hill, the road to Theydon Bois.

Cross the B172 to follow the trail over Copley Plain, and when the view to the right is over Dulsmead Hollow, be alert for a right turn off The Duchess Ride at **F.434989**. Fork right for the steep descent to Debden Slade, and climb equally steeply to cross Goldings Hill, another section of the A121.

Loughton Camp

Car-parks and bus stops mark the SW crossing. Continue SW for another steep descent to a sharp right bend to bridge Loughton Brook. Climb with Green Ride swinging left to revert to a southerly heading. When back on level terrain in the region of Loughton Camp turn right at a triangular junction **(G.421977)**. Proceed WNW to the Mount Pleasant car-park and a careful crossing of the A104.

There remains just a parish boundary to cross, a task much easier than a crossing of an A class road. Head westward to merge with another track. Turn acutely right on to this to round the eastern side of Epping Forest Conservation Centre and to make two crossings of a kerbed pathway for wheelchairs. The track swings left to emerge at the Cross Road junction overlooking Rushey Plain. The King's Oak is to the left, but you will probably have taken a short cut to be there and changed your shoes by now.

Pub Yarns

Epping is a Saxon upland dwelling.

Loughton Camp and Ambresbury Banks are roughly oval in shape and each covers about 6.5 acres. They are early Iron Age encampments.

On 6th May 1882 Queen Victoria dedicated 5,559 acres of Epping Forest to be managed for the enjoyment of the people for ever. Its first 100 years has seen off many an attack to diminish its acreage. It remains a colossal facility for citizens from miles around.

Before our civil war it was thought to extend over 60,000 acres. Felling timber for Naval ships demanded much oak, and the Enclosure Movement reduced the acreage to its present size. Today there are still pressures to shrink it further.

A feature of the Forest is pollarding, especially the beech trees. This practice is a sort of coppicing above ruminants' mouth height. Although the deer population in Essex is increasing, within Epping Forest the trend is reversed, probably by human disruption.

Epping Forest Conservation Centre was opened in European Conservation Year 1970.

Alfred Tennyson lived at Beech Hill in the 1830s. John Clare lived at High Beach and wrote some of his seminal works here before returning to Northamptonshire in 1841.

Speedway racing had an early stronghold at High Beach.

Walk 16: Henny Street's Henny Swan

The Henny Swan Inn has an idyllic situation with a beer garden beside the languid River Stour. When the gentle breeze parts the curtains of willow wands draping toward the reflective water, there are glimpses of rural scenes with cattle grazing safely on Suffolk's side of the river.

Some motorists have chanced upon the Swan, enjoyed a meal there, and attempted to return another day, only to forget the way. The combined parish council for Middleton, Henny and Twinstead does not have to worry with major roads, and the communities in its care do well without them.

How to get there

Depart from the A604 main road in Halstead and use the A131 to Sudbury. The approach to Sudbury is down Ballingdon Hill. Turn right at the bottom before getting too far in Suffolk. The country road winds through Middleton, with only Hall Farm to notice nearby, and gets even narrower as Henny Street is approached. The road bisects the Swan's beer garden, map reference 155TL879384.

Buses	None noticed
Trains	Sudbury station and taxi or bicycled connection!

What is there?

The hamlet of Henny Street comprises two junctions of country lanes, a sturdy footbridge over the picturesque River Stour as a link with Suffolk, some superb cottages, Mill House, Street Farmhouse, and Greatham Farm. A red mail box and a telephone kiosk., Livestock and arable fields complete the rural scene.

The Henny Swan Inn thrives in this setting because it sells good Greene King beer and good food all served well enough to attract visitors to this enchanting place. There is a pleasant restaurant and flora-abundant garden as well as the riverside garden. Parking is for patrons only. Alternative parking may be found on the verge by the church and parish room.

Walk details

Walking distance	7 kms (4.3 miles) needing about 105 minutes to stroll
Ordnance Survey maps	Landranger 155 Bury St Edmunds & Sudbury
	Pathfinder 1052 Halstead and Nayland
Paths used	Great Henny 10, 8, 2, 13, 22, 24, 28, 21
	Little Henny 5, 3.
District Council	Braintree

The Walk

From the Swan doorway face the river and turn left and left again by

LITTLE HENNY

HENNY STREET

START

Henny
Swan
Inn

Street
Farm

Applecroft

fieldedge
paths

Brookside
diversions

Thorncroft

River Stour

Midfield path

Parish
Room

Little Hickbush

driveway

drive
cum
bridle
way

GREAT HENNY

Fenn
Farm

Gt Hickbush
re-instated path

banktop
path

paddocks

Loshes Meadow
Nature Reserve

RTG
149

WALKING DISTANCE: 7 kms

Schematic map: not to scale

16

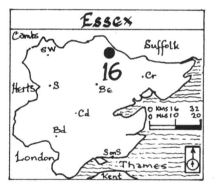

The Henny
Swan Inn
Great Henny
CO10 7LS

☎ 0787
269238

Day	Snacks		Meals	
	L,N	E,S	L,N	E,S
Sn	✓		✓	
M	✓	✓	✓	✓
T	✓	✓	✓	✓
W	✓	✓	✓	✓
Th	✓	✓	✓	✓
F	✓	✓	✓	✓
St	✓	✓	✓	✓

Walk Profile

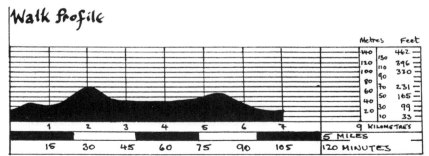

Henny Cottage. Rise with the little lane to its first big bend right, and leave to go left on bridleway 10. Head southward until a gap in the right-hand hedge allows a junction with a footpath.

Sometimes a permissive alternative to the mid-field path comes into operation. It follows the hedge to the ford level and goes right brookside upstream to the cartbridge.

Enter Little Henny by going left over the bridge and follow the ditch towards Applecroft Farm. Where a field boundary joins the other side of the ditch, the path should turn WNW, but again the permissive alternative along the field edge may provide better walking than tramping down a growing crop.

Either way, the path passes northside of Applecroft Farm to join the splendid path 3 down from Middleton cross-paths (**H.868384**). Go southward over the bridge and veer right by the hedge to stay to the west of the steading. A single sleeper footbridge connects with the next field where the eastern hedge again steers the path, this time to a stile in to a paddock.

Great Henny Church

Back in Great Henny, follow the eastern fence up to Thorncroft Farm and exit by the stile under the two oak trees and get east of the barns and transformer. Climb the field-edge path up to a lane northside of St Mary's church.

Turn right and pass the lych gate to follow the lane out to Great Henny Parish Room. Go left and fork right on to Fenn Farm drive which is also a bridleway.

Head southwards down the drive to keep the farmhouse and garage on the left and larger buildings on the right. Swing left to get to the east of the large lake and turn left to have paddock rails on the left-hand side. The ESE path follows the line of the valley over a stile and along a field-edge to the SE corner where a complicated stile allows access to the next field.

There appears to be a choice of path, either public by the field-edge on top of the bank, or private within the shrubbery of Loshes Meadow Nature Reserve at the bank foot. The two unite by the huge pylon with a three-way stretch of cables (**J.872370**).

Hickbush Country

Exit on the Henny side of Loshhouse bridge and turn left uphill N, under the cables to the bank end right. Climb to walk the bank top path through to the next pylon and beyond on a mid-field path etched through the crop to the SW corner of Great Hickbush garden. Turn left beside the garden to join the drive which is shared, together with its views, out via Little Hickbush to a road bend.

An avenue of oak trees beckons a right turn down the country lane and swings eastwards to a path junction left (K.876377). A causeway of grass NNE connects with another tarmac lane. Go right to join Henny Street at Greatham Farm parish notice board. Face the traffic coming from Sudbury to pass between Street Farmhouse and Mill House to Henny Swan. Please remove or cover any outdoor footwear before going indoors.

Pub Yarns

Otters are practically extinct in the Stour valley. There is no need for otter hounds to evacuate them. Hunters have been concerned to keep their sport active, but the numbers have declined. Poachers may have been after pelts, or our changing arable and domestic practices, or even changes to the climate, may contribute to the loss of otters. The Mammal Society is working to maintain some of these river-loving creatures within our shores.

The Sudbury branch railway covers twelve miles from the main line at Marks Tey. It was built about 150 years ago and has survived a threat of closure through the last three decades. Henny Street is between stations but it is still reassuring to see the Sprinters travel through the valley.

Walk 17: Elmdon's King's Head

The large irregular shaped parish of Elmdon has its boundary interlocked with Wenden Lofts like a jigsaw puzzle. It is situated on the chalky outliers of the Chiltern Hills, pressing against the Cambridgeshire border, and nudging against Chrishall's spot height of 147 metres - the highest place in Essex - by Pickerton Green and Oldfield Grove.

It is a village of several settlements. This walk leaves the main one, by the picturesque 1870 St Nicholas' church, and goes through other hamlets and parishes.

How to get there

Leave the M11 by junction 10 and use the A505 SSW to bear left on to the B1368 at Flints Cross. Join the B1339 in Barley, leaving Hertfordshire E via Cambridgeshire. Rise to Great Chishill and dip to the Essex county sign. Two miles on, turn acutely left at a junction signposted ELMDON. Climb by Wenden Lofts to Elmdon church by the triangular road junction with the King's Head at the beginning of Heydon Lane, map reference 154TL461396.

Buses	Services 31, 41, 42, 62 with westward links stronger than those in to Essex.
Trains	Wendens Ambo (Audley End station) on the West Anglian line with taxi or bicycle connections.

What is there?

Elmdon cares for its village environment, judging by the well-kept trees, gardens and fieldpaths in the area. A village enterprise to reinforce the impression is the nature trail beginning off Kings Lane complete with sponsored leaflet obtainable from a box near the weather station.

The King's Head is the village pub with bed and breakfast option. Greene King, Ind Cocpe and Tetley ales are sold and there is a restaurant and garden to enjoy. It has a good car-park, with alternative car parking at the nature trail or road verge parking at Duddenhoe End.

Walk details

Walking distance	8 kms (5 miles) requiring about 120 minutes to stroll
Ordnance Survey maps	Landranger 154 Cambridge & Newmarket
	Pathfinder 1050 Saffron Walden
Paths used	Elmdon 14, 15, 16,19, 20, 17, 12. Chrishall 13, 14, 24.
	Wenden Lofts 1, 3, 18, 4, 16, 17
District Council	Uttlesford

The Walk

Head southwards on the footway of Essex Hill, turning right by the telephone kiosk on to an unmade lane to confront Shepherds' Hay. Fork left up Kings Lane and re-join Essex Hill temporarily to pass the front of Carpenters Cottage and turn right again opposite Wallis Farm and use the path skirting the recreation ground.

Trace the copper beech hedge southwards to a double stiled crossing of a track from Lofts Hall set amid high-standards of husbandry in which the public pathways are not neglected. They are in a splendid setting, overlooked by St Dunstan's church tower. At the lower three-way fence junction, a stile admits access to a footbridge (**L.460383**).

Duddenhoe End

Head SE on a grassy headland with a hedge on the left-hand side. Cross the track, and bend right by a newly planted hedgeline out to a bridge over Wenden Water alongside the B1039 road.

Cross the road going slightly right to the avenue of chestnut trees. Leave the valley via the path under the trees and continue southwards by the tall hedge to cross School Lane and Elmdon's Upper Pond Street. The mid-field path crosses a culvert bridge and climbs steadily to pass between garden hedges and joins a bend in Duddenhoe End road (**M.462367**).

Chiswick Hall Moat

Pass right through Duddenhoe End, going right again beyond the Woodman to the footpath beginning by a transformer on a pole (**N.459367**). Slope off N downhill to the bridge at the second convex hedge corner. Continue the mid-field direction across the smaller field to a bridleway bridge and approach the corner of Mead Bushy Wood.

Now back in Wenden Lofts, pass the southern and western sides of the woodland to locate a second bridleway bridge over the boundary brook with Chrishall. Climb the mid-field bridleway to the moated Chiswick Hall (**Q.450375**). The worn route is north of the steading, although the mapped route is over the moat bridge and on the drive.

Descend the drive to cross the B1039 road and then the Wenden Water footbridge to climb by a vestigial hedge up to Chrishall's Holy Trinity church (**R.451385**). Go right by the southern sides of the Vicarage and Park Wood and the path becomes a headland dipping to a left turn.

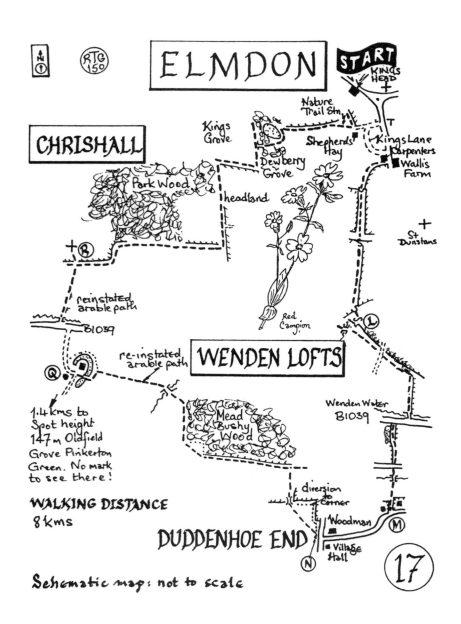

ELMDON

START KINGS HEAD

CHRISHALL

Nature Trail Stn

Kings Grove

Shepherds Hay

Kings Lane Carpenters Wallis Farm

Park Wood

Dewberry Grove

headland

St Dunstans

reinstated arable path

Red Campion

B1039

re-instated arable path

WENDEN LOFTS

1.4 kms to Spot height 147 m Oldfield Grove Pinkerton Green. No mark to see there!

Wenden Water B1039

Mead Bushy Wood

WALKING DISTANCE
8 kms

diversion to corner

Woodman

DUDDENHOE END

Village Hall

17

Schematic map: not to scale

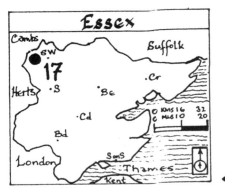

The King's Head

Heydon Lane

Elmdon

Essex   CB

☎   0763
      838358

Day	Snacks		Meals	
	Ln	Eg	Ln	Eg
Sn	✓	✓	✓	✓
M	✓	✓	✓	✓
T	✓	✓	✓	✓
W	✓	✓	✓	✓
Th	✓	✓	✓	✓
F	✓	✓	✓	✓
St	✓	✓	✓	✓

Walk Profile

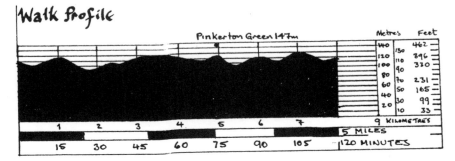

Nature Trail

Rise with the track which becomes a path approaching the eastern edge of Park Wood. Cross the footbridge in the corner and go right along the field-edge around to a Nature Trail arrow between Dewberry and Kings Groves. Pass east and north of the ponds to use the headland across to the weather station in the Nature Trail car-park by Shepherds' Hay. Rejoin Essex Hill going left to the King's Head. Removal of mud from footwear is appreciated.

Pub Yarns

Some paths used on this walk are by the Icknield Way, Britain's oldest known highway which connects the Peddars Way to the Ridgeway.

This highest corner of Essex is on an extension of the Chiltern Hills. The chalky land was once a downland, and only changed to arable in recent centuries. The stone curlew and the corncrake both flourished here as did many flowers and butterflies no longer seen in the vicinity.

The Linking Environment and Farm project is developing demonstration areas to inform the public about the safety of chemicals used to produce optimum yields. The Elmdon Nature Trail is part of this project.

King's Head, Lane and Grove are named after a believed visit by King Charles II to a hunting lodge in the area.

The Hamlet church at Duddenhoe End is a former barn and is one of the rare thatched churches in the county.

Walk 18: Chigwell Row's Two Brewers

Chigwell Row occupies high land between the rivers Roding and Rom. Building development has expanded the Havering side of the Row, but Hainault Forest provides an important green lung on much of the ridge. The Two Brewers is close to this remnant of the ancient Forest of Essex, now alongside the London Boroughs of Havering and Redbridge.

How to get there

Leave the Eastern Avenue A12 road for the A112 by the Moby Dick and travel northwards on Whalebone Lane to the top of the second hill where traffic lights control the junction with the B173 road. Filter right here by All Saints' church on to Lambourne Road, passing the Maypole to find the Two Brewers on the left-hand side, map reference 177TQ468936.

Buses	Services 8, 89 infrequent
Trains	Grange Hill station (London Underground) one mile SW of All Saints church along B 173.

What is there?

Chigwell Row is a busy urban thoroughfare bordering a huge open space backed by the trees of Hainault Common. East of the Two Brewers car-park is a primary school opposite which a car-park caters for many visitors to this part of Hainault Forest Park.

The Two Brewers is 300 years old and its concrete-faced walls cover very strong crossed oak saplings filled with daub. This friendly Whitbread pub seems set to serve for another 300 years with its restaurant and garden.

Walk details

Walking distance	10 kms (6.25 miles) needing about 150 minutes to stroll
Ordnance Survey maps	Landranger 177 East London
	Pathfinder 1141 for Hainault Forest
Paths used	Chigwell Row 107, 102
	Lambourne 20, 19, 17, 5, 16, 11, 12, 14.
District Council	Epping Forest

The Walk

Use Lambourne Road's sidewalk by the primary school and cross to The Common. The central walk across this broad greensward heads for a notch in the treeline of Cabin Hill. When on the bare earth between the blocks of trees, continue on Cavill's Walk up and over the crosstracks by the holly leaves on Cabin Hill **(S.480939)**, to descend the eastern side

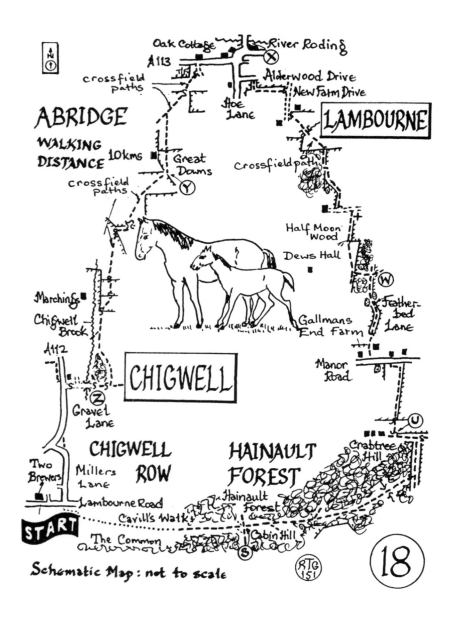

Oak Cottage
A113
River Roding
crossfield paths
Aldorwood Drive
New Farm Drive
Hoe Lane
ABRIDGE
LAMBOURNE
WALKING DISTANCE 10kms
Great Doms
Crossfield path
crossfield paths
Y
Half Moon Wood
Dews Hall
W
Feather-bed Lane
Marchings
Chigwell Brook
A112
Gallmans End Farm
Manor Road
Z
Gravel Lane
CHIGWELL
U
CHIGWELL ROW
HAINAULT FOREST
Crabtree Hill
Two Brewers
Millers Lane
Lambourne Road
Cavill's Walk
Hainault Forest
The Common
Cabin Hill
S
START
RTG 151
18

Schematic Map: not to scale

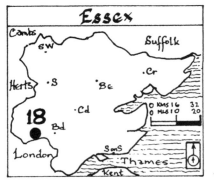

The Two Brewers
57 Lambourne Rd
Chigwell Row
Essex

081
501-1313

Day	Snacks		Meals	
	Lh	Eg	Lh	Eg
Sn	✓			
M	✓			
T	✓			
W	✓			
Th	✓			
F	✓			
St	✓			

Walk Profile

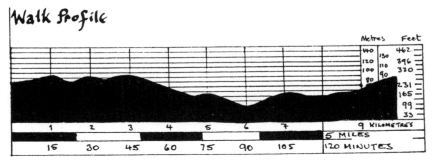

parallel with a bridleway and the occasionally visible southern boundary fence. Cross the stream and climb to the eastern boundary track and share the courtesy bridlepath to the corner of Crabtree Hill. Three dwellings abound the forest here. Upside of the eastern one, a stile indicates a northward path **(U.487945)**.

Lambourne

Cross the pasture to the gap by the hedge junction and continue along a field-edge to exit on to Manor Road by a T-junction of wires at a stilted transformer. Face oncoming traffic as far as Gallmans End Farm where a bridleway allows the northward journey to proceed. Keep the main building on the right-hand side and fencing of Featherbed Lane steers the path downhill beyond the ponds to the left-hand coppice.

A path goes right to the scenic Roding valley. Ignore it **(W.480957)**. Go left instead, through the copse to the grazing before Dews Hall.

Go right to chamfer off the NE corner and locate a stile-under-brambles. A field-edge path connects the stile to St Mary & All Saints' church at Lambourne. Go west along the drive to the white gate. Turn right on a path hugging the garden fence around to Soapley Wood.

Abridge

Change sides of the hedge via a broken bridge and continue downhill under the thorn canopy to the bottom stile. Cross the grazing NW to the footbridge SW of Alder Wood. The path is etched in the grasses through to New Farm. Go down the drive to the beginning of Abridge's housing on the left. A left turn skirts the southern side of the gardens until opposite an isolated tree. Turn right between fencing to emerge by 36 Alderwood Drive. To the left is Hoe Lane. Connect with it to continue down to the B172 bridge over the River Roding **(X.466970)**.

Back through Abridge pass the White Hart and following Silver Street by the Blue Boar around to A113 London bound road by The Maltsters and Log Cabin Cafe. Opposite Oak Cottage a path begins from a stile set back by Dashwell House.

Pass the transformer on the right and head southerly across the grasses to a stile. Maintain direction in the next field, forking left to stay east of

Great Downs Farm buildings and caravans to reach the stile by a gas marker (**Y.465961**).

Chigwell Brook

Good views across Chigwell Brook valley may be seen from the stile. Head across the grazing SSW via a convex hedge corner to a stile and footbridge waymarked yellow in the lower hedge. Once across go right to the hedge junction, climb to the next field and continue southwards heading for the tip of a fir tree which is all that can be seen of Marchings Farm until the brow is crested.

Stiles mark the route through a set of railed fences to the bottom SW corner where two more stiles transfer the path to the western edge of an arable field beside Chigwell Brook.

To The Ridge

Proceed upstream beyond the theoretical bridging place until at the path junction by a cart bridge of sleeper-logs and a weather-boarded dwelling (**Z.464949**). Turn right over the brook to use the stiled exit to the A112.

Continue uphill, first on the grassy sidewalk of Gravel Lane and then facing downward traffic on Millers Lane. Lambourne Road is at the top of the hill and sustenance at The Two Brewers is a short way WSW along the sidewalk. Please remove or cover muddy outdoor boots before going indoors.

Pub Yarns

Hainault Forest provided timber for ship building and produced charcoal for much of the Thameside industry.

At least one prize fight was reported in 1828.

Chigwell is the Saxon settlement of Cingheuuella.

John Arnold improved the action of time pieces, in much the same way as John Harrison did, to assist navigation at sea.

Sally Gunnell, winner of the some fine four hundred metres hurdles races, hails from Chigwell.

Walk 19: Clavering's Fox & Hounds

The moated site of Clavering Castle is secure in the valley of the River Stort beside the church and at the parish centre. Off centre are several hamlets like Stickling Green, Roast Green, Starlings Green and Deers Green, nearly a dozen in all, set in the Essex-Hertfordshire border countryside. The river parts the rolling fields in two and this Walk samples both sides.

How to get there

Depart from the M11 at junction 8 to use the A120 westwards and the B1383 road northwards to pass through Stansted Mountfitchet and enter Newport. Beyond The Hercules Inn, and before the pinnacles of St Mary the Virgin's church tower, resume a westward direction on the B1038 road which passes the Fox & Hounds on the approach to Clavering centre, map reference 167TL476319

Buses	Service 302 to Stansted Mountfitchet and some days service 11 to Newport.
Trains	Newport on the West Anglia line.

What is there?

Clavering's village centre has cottage rose scent trapped under thatched eaves set beside fords of rippling water. A pump and a Guildhall embellish the moated castle site beside a seventeenth century mansion, The Bury. The buttressed tower of St Mary's and St Clement's rises high to oversee the rooftops nestled in the valley.

The Fox & Hounds is the nearest village pub to the core settlement. It is a free house selling Benskins ales and lunchtime snacks. There is also plenty of outdoor seating and an adequate car-park for patrons. Alternative parking is on the verge of Rickling Road above Poor Bridge.

Walk details

Walking distance	7 kms (4.4 miles) needing about 105 minutes to stroll
Ordnance Survey maps	Landranger 167 Chelmsford & Harlow
	Pathfinder 1050 Saffron Walden
Paths used	Clavering 50, 4, 51, 5, 68. Berden 58, 3.
District Council	Uttlesford

The Walk

From the Fox & Hounds head SSE along The Druce beside the river for two furlongs where a stile permits the riverside walk to continue but the chalky track swings left uphill. Climb Chalkpit Lane to obtain views across the valley from the top. They include the remains two sail-less tower windmills out by Roast Green.

Under the pyloned wires continue to the lane junction (A.486313) and turn right between the high hedges of Highfield Lane and link with Rickling Road.

Go right to face any traffic coming from Berden as the country lane dips to Poor Bridge over the Stort and rises to a crossroads. Walk straight on to the cross-path at the far end of the cypress hedge. Turn right on the headland which swings left with the hedgeline under the wires and across a bridge to the next field.

Berden Ford

Now on a bank about a storey higher than the left-hand field, proceed until a tank on block pillars is reached near a ford in Berden **(B.467303)**.

Turn right up Parsonage Lane to re-enter Clavering and look for path 51. A right turn at the next field boundary has a hedge on the right-hand side of path 5. Pass the ditch boundary and locate a bridge for the needed but missing cross-path.

Explore along the hedgeline for a further furlong to behold a reinstated metre-wide path through the crop about a furlong off the expected line of path 51.

Re-aligned Path

The reinstated line joins with the junction of paths 53 and 54 at **C.473310**. To re-connect with path 51, follow the worn path across the plank bridge and turn NNW. Walk the field-edge with ditch on left then step over left at D.471313.

Now back on the proper path 51, use it over the mid-field section to the garden fences of Pelham Road cottages. These fences steer the path out to the triangular green by the much photographed Guildhall which is passed to enter the churchyard of St Mary and St Clement.

Ramparts

Northwest of the church is the moat with path 68 running along its top southern rampart. Go right to the Post House and left down Middle Street to the footbridge beside the ford. Turn ESE along Langley Road to merge with the B1038 by the Stort bridge in front of the Fox & Hounds.

WALKING DISTANCE 7kms

Schematic Map not to scale.

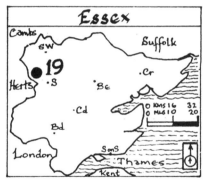

The Fox & Hounds

High Street

Clavering

Essex.

☎ 0799
550321

Day	Snacks		Meals	
	Lh	Eg	Lh	Eg
Sn	✓			
M	✓			✓
T	✓			✓
W	✓			✓
Th	✓			✓
F	✓			✓
St	✓			✓

Walk Profile

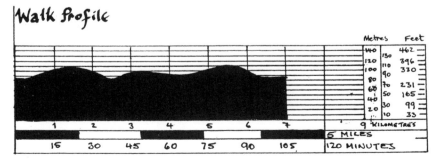

Outdoor muddy boots should be washed in the ford, swapped for clean ones, or covered with plastic bags before going indoors.

Pub Yarns

Clavering means a Saxon place where clover grew.

At the heart of the village is the old baronial castle of Robert Fitz Wymarc. The beautiful church porch is said to have been built with materials from the castle.

A vicar of Clavering in 1782 is alleged to have sermonised against the poor for being too taken up with warding off starvation to attend to their spiritual matters.

Sometimes Clavering wins awards in the Best Kept Village competitions.

Thatching was one of those crafts fostered by the Rural Industries Bureau way back in 1966 when England was winning soccer's World Cup. Some of these old crafts have developed markets in the modern age, and the demand for thatch repairs and replacement as seen around Clavering, shows a lusty survival. A good thatch, some ten inches thick, should last for twenty years.

Blacksmithing, especially the farriers' work, is another craft surviving rural development. The increase in horse riding brings about a demand for more and better bridleways too.

There may be less demand for wood-carving and for basket-making, at the moment, but their skills should not become extinct as long as there are some craftpersons clinging to livelihoods. Will the windmills be revived?

Walk 20: Belchamp Otten's Red Lion

A cluster of three villages prefixed Belchamp overlook Suffolk across the Stour valley from their arable acres of north Essex. From west to east they are St Paul, Otten and Walter, and this Walk uses paths in all three parishes.

Belchamp St Paul has the largest nucleated settlement and Belchamp Otten is relatively scattered, as is the other Belchamp - Walter which claims Belchamp Hall, the model TV home of Lovejoy's Lady Jane.

How to get there

Leave the A604 Cambridge - Colchester main road at Birdbrook's Baythorne End to use the A1092 in Suffolk as far as Clare. Use Ashen Road to re-cross the river and turn left up Hickford Hill, bearing right to pass St Andrew's church. At the southern end of Church Street turn left for Belchamp Otten and find The Red Lion signposted right in Fowes Lane, map referenced 155TL798414.

Buses	A Tuesday Thursday and Saturday connection to Sudbury.
Trains	Sudbury station connected via taxi, bicycle or, on certain days, bus.

What is there?

Otten is a rural community with its largest cluster of buildings along the street containing St Ethelbert's and All Saints' church. The local primary school is at Belchamp St Paul passed on this Walk, and the secondary school is by Castle and Sible Hedingham.

The Red Lion although a cosy country pub competes for local and visiting trade very professionally offering a full pub service of meals, Greene King ales, and a restaurant. Parking is for patrons only. Alternative parking is on the verge of Hobart Road near "G".

Walk details

Walking distance	9 kms (5.6 miles) needing about 135 minutes to stroll.
Ordnance Survey maps	Landranger 155 Bury St Edmunds & Sudbury
	Pathfinders 1029 Sudbury & Lavenham
	1028 Haverhill & Clare
Paths used	Belchamp Otten 17, 18, 15, 3, 2, 11, 30.
	Belchamp Walter 5, 3. Belchamp St Paul 10, 22.
District Council	Braintree

The Walk

Go to the north end of Fowes Lane and turn right on a footpath going by a farmhouse and then with a hedge on the left-hand side as far as a

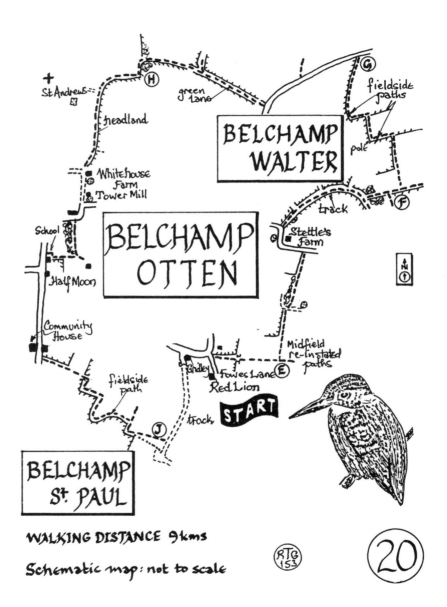

St Andrews
green lane
H
headland
fieldside paths
BELCHAMP WALTER
pole
Whitehouse Farm
Tower Mill
track
F
School
BELCHAMP OTTEN
Stettle's Farm
Half Moon
N
Community House
Midfield re-instated paths
fieldside path
Findley
Fowes Lane
Red Lion
E
START
track
J
BELCHAMP St. PAUL

WALKING DISTANCE 9kms

Schematic map: not to scale

RTG 153

20

Fowes Lane

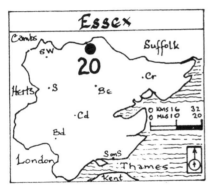

Essex

Cambs
SW
20
Suffolk
.Cr
Herts .S .Bc
.Cd
Bd
London
SonS
Thames
Kent

0 kms 16 32
0 Miel0 20

The Red Lion
Fowes Lane
Belchamp Otten
Essex.

0787
277537

Day	Snacks		Meals	
	Ln	Es	Ln	Es
Sn	✓	✓	✓	✓
M	✓	✓	✓	✓
T	✓	✓	✓	✓
W	✓	✓	✓	✓
Th	✓	✓	✓	✓
F	✓	✓	✓	✓
St	✓	✓	✓	✓

Walk Profile

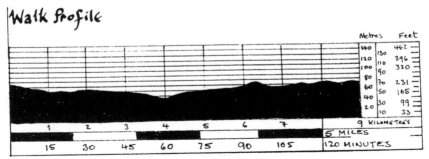

	Metres	Feet
	140	462
	130	
	120	396
	110	
	100	330
	90	
	80	231
	70	
	60	165
	50	
	40	99
	30	
	20	33
	10	

1 2 3 4 5 6 7   9 KILOMETRES

5 MILES

15 30 45 60 75 90 105   120 MINUTES

footbridge. Path 17 becomes a reinstated line heading for a gap in the further bank, but does not reach the gap.

Turn left instead mid-field(**E.802413**)when aligned with the convex bank corner left. Move to that corner and walk the field-edge as far as the track junction. Go south of the tree belt by the track and continue along the hedge-side to join Puttock End Road, going left to round the corner by Stettle's Farm.

Green Lane

Off the next bend veer right on to the bridleway curving down by a pond and around to the right where the vehicle marks enter a fieldgate and the hoof prints bear left uphill. Go between high hedges to a staggered crossing of paths (**F.812414**).

Use the left turn, invisible across a narrow field to the convex hedge corner where another path is joined. Head north-eastwards along the rough head!and path and use the bridge in the hedge to turn left in the next field. Round the corner by the pole and enter the next field via a gap marked with elm logs.

Bevingdon Bridleway

Another left turn allows a repeat of the corner manoeuvre on an equally rough and narrow headland path. Follow the hedge line again as far as Hobart Road (**G.821421**).

Face traffic oncoming from Belchamp Otten and dip with the road to bridleway 3 going off right. Rise with the green lane between high hedges. The banks get lower as the lane gains height. Stay left at the fork of lanes even though this means going left of the left-hand hedge to get clear of a blockage.

Belchamp St Paul

The high hedgeline terminates at a small copse (**H.808431**) commanding good views over the valley of a Belchamp Brook tributary stream. Follow the bank left and round the corner to be opposite St Andrew's and above the treatment plant.

A grassy track hugs the hedgeline through to Whitehouse Farm. Pass the pond and use the concrete road to Tower Mill Road corner. Maintain direction over both road bends, and continue on path 11 until it bends left. Go right around the corner of the woodland on an excellent path which enters Belchamp St Paul via the Nature Reserve at the rear of the Primary School.

Community House

Left along Vicarage Road pass The Half Moon Inn to walk the green SW as far as Community House. Turn left on to a footpath beside the old military vehicles of Lamberts Farm, and when the left-hand hedge turns away along the parish boundary, continue ahead on a reinstated path through to the footbridge over the field divider.

The right-hand hedgeline now steers the path through two concave bends and then it is joined by a path from the left. From the junction, maintain the south-easterly direction on a reinstated path heading up to an oak tree in a hedge end (J.794415).

Two tracks lead off a large concreted area. Use the one leading NE and join Otten Road by Gridley.Turn right again to find the Red Lion in Fowes Lane. Muddy footwear should be removed or covered before entering the pub please.

PUB YARNS

Belchamp is said to derive from beauchamps meaning beautiful fields. Otten means the place of the son of Otto, Walter was the home of the De Vere family in 1086, and St Paul is a reference to part of the village being given to St Paul's Cathedral in 931.

Essex once had a thriving straw plaiting industry organised on the outwork system and cottagers of all three Belchamps were involved.

St Ethelbert and All Saints church in Belchamp Otten retains some box pews. St.Andrew's church in Belchamp St Paul has a 15th century tower. The superb Community House was given to the village by the Bryce family.

This village amid vast arable acres that once grazed many more cows, used to excite its dull Decembers with an annual cattle fair at Cole Green.

MEANDERINGS THROUGH VERDANT VALLEYS

There are eleven walks in this chapter, distributed around good pubs in the catchments of the Chelmer, Blackwater and Colne rivers. They are spread to show rivers in their young, middle and older age stages.

ALERT

Our rivers are important as drains to take away surplus water, and as suppliers of fresh clean water. Their upkeep is an ever-increasing tax burden. A riverside walk is almost a riverside patrol; whilst enjoying the ramble one has to be alert to any signs of ill-health with the river and be ready to report it to the River Authority. Dead roach, rudd, perch or dace are a sign that something is wrong.

PLEASURE

The sounds and reflections of water make charming habitats for many forms of wildlife. Many ramblers, like anglers, are interested in water and fish. Vigilant ramblers may see herons levering their way up from a bank to slowly flap away to a new fishing spot, or grebes re-appearing from an underwater food-search. The squawk of moorhen mixes with the warbler's warble and the lark's lament. Silently an orange-tip or Essex skipper butterfly may flutter by to add decoration to a scintillating scene.

PONDS

Many old farm ponds have gone, but many new farm reservoirs and old gravel pit lagoons compensate for their loss.

VALLEY PATHS

Actual riverbank paths are rarely continuous in the soft clays of Essex. Streams feeding the rivers cause too many swampy interruptions to such routes, and our forbears established our paths on drier terrain.

All defined rights-of-way should be clearly visible with at least one metre width of walkable surface. Headland paths should be 1.5 metres wide.

Walk 21: Thaxted's Star

Handsome Thaxted sits proudly above the young river Chelmer. It is like some mainland European settlements inasmuch as it has a strongly clustered development that does not straggle unduly in to the surrounding arable countryside. It was one of the most prosperous towns in the county 500 years ago and the tall spire of St John the Baptist, Our Lady, and St Lawrence parish church, seen from miles around, serves as a reminder of that prosperity. Another architectural gem of Thaxted is the three-storeyed Guildhall, with open timbers on three sides of the ground floor.

How to get there

Depart from the M 11 at junction 8 and use the A120 eastwards to Dunmow, filtering left in to Dunmow to connect with B184 north to Thaxted. The Star is in Mill End, which is the B184 by its junction with Park Street on the approach to the picturesque Guildhall, map reference 167TL613308.

Buses	Service 313 Great Dunmow - Saffron Walden weekdays
Trains	Nearest station Newport. Connect by taxi or bicycle.

What is there?

Thaxted: a settlement that once was large in comparison with others in the land, has retained a similar size, but other places have grown to have populations ten times greater. Thaxted has retained benefits but what, if anything, has it lost by not expanding so rapidly?

The Star has a welcome for visitors, and morris dancing is not unknown in the vicinity - always the sign of a good pub. Adnams ales are stocked and there is a restaurant. The car parking is for patrons. An alternative free park is signed off Town Street in Margaret Street via The Tanyard and Weaverhead Lane.

Walk details

Walking distance	8 kms (5 miles) requiring about 120 minutes to stroll
Ordnance Survey maps	Landranger 167 Chelmsford & Harlow
	Pathfinder 1051 Thaxted & Sible Hedingham
	1075 Great Dunmow · & Braintree
Paths used	Thaxted 49, 50, 79, 46, 32, 27, 30,
District Council	Uttlesford

The Walk

From the front door of The Star approach the Guildhall, and then use Stoney Lane to find entry to the churchyard path, rising still to be below the west face of the tower next to Bolford Street. Without mingling with the traffic, turn left on the churchyard shingle by the seat, and leave

Copthall Lane

brookside path

midfield path

Sampford Road

Guildhall
B184

Wedow Road

Mill End
The Star
B1051

START

Butchers
Holly Oak Arms
Farm

field edge paths

**BARDFIELD
END GREEN**

Stepover

THAXTED

headland

Plummers Wood

headland
Parkstyle Cottage   B1051

headland

Brook Side diversion greensward

River Chelmer

WALKING DISTANCE 8kms

Greenways

**RICHMOND'S
GREEN**

MONK STREET

midfield path
Stepover

(21)

Folly Mill

Farmhouse Inn

field edge paths

RTG 154

Schematic map: not to scale

The Star
Mill End
Thaxted
Essex.

☎ 0371
830368

Day	Snacks		Meals	
	Ln	Eg	Ln	Eg
Sn	✓	✓	✓	✓
M	✓	✓	✓	✓
T	✓	✓	✓	✓
W	✓	✓	✓	✓
Th	✓	✓	✓	✓
F	✓	✓	✓	✓
St	✓	✓	✓	✓

Walk Profile

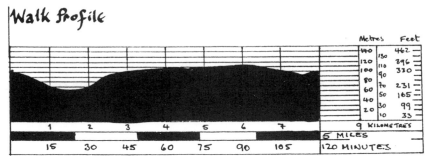

southwards by the almshouses and the picnic site by John Webb's restored windmill of 1804 to find the open country. Head southwards on a grassy path sloping down to Stan Brook with the river Chelmer a field away on the right-hand side.

Monk Street

Join the B1051 road going left by Parkstyle Cottage and cross to the handrailed footbridge. In the field a broad brookside greensward serves as the path around to the confluence of Stan Brook with the Chelmer. Bridges, stiles and waymarks aid the path's riverside passage through three more fields to Folly Mill **(K.609288)**.

Rise with Folly Mill Lane left under the arches of mixed hawthorn, oak and hazel hedgerow trees to Monk Street. Go left by the Farmhouse Inn and cross the B184 to the field-edge path climbing eastwards with its hedge on the left-hand side.

At the top **(L.620290)** there is a ditch to step over and a flat field to traverse diagonally ENE towards the dwelling Greenways. Share the opening to the road with path 80 and turn right to find the red mail box at Richmond's Green.

Richmond's Green

Fork left on the drive going beyond the gate to the pond. Turn left by an old fuel pump and use the headland N beyond the buildings and cross a field to a T-junction of overhead wires. Go right and left with the track to pass to the west of Plummers Wood and continue one field beyond the trees to where the track bends right. Ignore the bend and stay with the left-hand boundary for a few paces seeking a bridge to swap sides of the ditch **(M.626302)**.

Step over if no bridge is in place (because the next cross-ditch is deeper) and stay to the west of a junction of ditches before a bridge allows a swap back to the eastern side. Turn left to stay by the side of the ditch and go right on the headland towards the camping site.

Bardfield End Green

Turn right again and find a gap from the concave corner which threads the path beside The Butchers' Arms on to the boundary of Bardfield End Green cricket field. Pass the pavilion and turn left on the road to pass Holly Oak Farm and another red mail box to find the acute right turn on to Sampford Road. Walk the roadside ENE for 2 minutes to find a footpath waymarked left.(N.625309).

Path 27 offers a delightful passage NNW in to the Copthall valley. Turn left at the bottom on a green lane leading to a harder surface by the woodland. From a sharp left-hand bend, continue ahead on a fieldside path with the stream on the left-hand side. Two streams merge and each has a footbridge (Q.617314). Cross the right-hand one to be north side of the incised brooks and walk the field-edge SW until the worn path diverges to link with 10 Brook View, an estate of newer houses. Go left on to Wedow Road, and left again on Weaverhead Lane. A right turn on to Tanyard's narrow sidewalk leads to the junction of Orange Street, Park Street, Town Street and Mill End.

Cover muddy footwear with plastic bags before entering to avoid depositing chunks of boulder clay in the pub. Some other guests may wonder which sect or cult you follow, or whether you are out of work unable to afford real shoes. Matching plastic bags from Boots are apt; a pair of Harrods bags just swanky!

Pub Yarns

Have you ever eaten sweets from Lee's of Thaxted? George Lee set up a sweet factory over a hundred years ago in Mill End, using horses to distribute glass jars of sweets to the surrounding districts. The railway connections were helpful between 1913 and 1952.

Local firms such as Lee's, and Cowell & Cooper's engineering works in Weaverhead Close, act as reminders of the busy medieval times when Thaxted was an established wool town and had pride in its cutlery industry. Profits from these trades helped to create the flying buttresses and 200 foot spire of the large church which dominates the local landscape still.

In 1881 a fire in Bolford Street fanned by strong winds quickly caused much damage to the tightly packed thatched houses.

Walk 22: Stebbing's Kings Head

Stebbing Brook contributes to the Chelmer river. The fold of land made by the passage of the brook is commanded by the village of Stebbing. Both the castle and the church and consequently, most of the cottages are on the eastern bank. The other bank, west of the splendid mill, is relatively neglected.

Southeast of the parish is Stebbing Green, a large unspoilt grassy wilderness, which ironically will need strong administration to keep it that way for a few more centuries. At the moment it is the place where any cottage garden might be ready for chocolate box lid illustration.

How to Get There

Leave the M11 at junction 8 and use the A120 eastwards beyond Dunmow and up the hill to the water tower. Take the next minor road left signposted STEBBING and turn left at the church to find the Kings Head on the right-hand side of High Street, map reference 167TL662242:

Buses	Services 314, 315 & 316 combine to offer once each way trips to Dunmow on Wednesdays, Thursdays, Fridays and Saturdays plus Braintree on Wednesdays and Saturdays and Chelmsford on Fridays.
Trains	Nearest station Braintree and connect by bicycle or taxi.

What is there?

Stebbing is an attractive village, opened up for inspection along either side of a street stretching from Church End to Bran End. The inter-mix of buildings of various types is quite remarkable; and individually many a building will keep one's interest for too long a time if a walk is also contemplated. The church has a stone screen and a fine roof among its many attributes.

The Kings Head fully nestles in the scene. It is a freehouse selling Greene King and Tetley beers, plus meals and lunch time snacks. There is also a garden, a meeting room and facilities for disabled customers.

Walk details

Walking distance	7.6 kms (4.8 miles) needing 114 minutes to stroll
Ordnance Survey maps	Landranger 167 Chelmsford & Harlow
	Pathfinder 1075 Great Dunmow & Braintree
Paths used	Stebbing 42, 45, 46, 4, 2, 38, 10, 21. Lindsell 17, 18.
District Council	Uttlesford

The Walk

From the Kings Head move left down the narrowing High Street and up the hill to Church End. Enter the churchyard by the west gate and admire the fourteenth century St Mary the Virgin's church. Leave by the east gate and greens surrounding the picturesque cottages and face the Watchhouse Road traffic as far the left turn on to Whitehouse Lane, also signed for Lubber Hedges Lane, by the tennis courts.

Dingle

Where the lane swings right, keep straight ahead on Clay Lane byway to view the valley of Stebbing Brook off left which will be walked later. Pass Brick Kiln Farm and keep straight ahead downhill at the junction, looking for a gate and signpost to the west of the barn. Go right through the stile in the high-railed fencing and cross the grazing N heading for a bridge over a subsidiary stream to Stebbing Brook. Keep the stream on the right-hand side until beyond the clump of scrub foliage and then bear left up the rabbit-nibbled grasses of a convex sandy slope to a double stile at the crest (**R.659253**).

A wind fan wheel may be seen beyond the trees. Head N towards it gradually converging with the edge of the woodland spreading up from the splendid dingle on the left. The map shows path 46 going through it, but the bridge is hidden or missing. Maintain, N direction on a path now on the top eastern fringe of the wooded zone, descend N under the canopy as the woodland swings right with the valley. A footbridge gives egress to an arable field and a union with path 2 in the nearby SW corner (**S.660259**).

Lindsell

Path 2 appears to progress no further south or west. An additional path follows the northern hedge around to a green lane exit on to the B 1057 road opposite White Hart Cottage.

Beside the cottage is the concrete drive to Lashley Hall. Follow it until south of the Hall. Turn left on to a headland dipping in to a wooded valley. The path chamfers some corners, but the alternative edges are easier to walk, especially around the corner now dampened by a lagoon.

Go left in the valley to have the vegetation on the right-hand side. Turn right at the next headland and approach the cartbridge. Go left before crossing it and follow the ditch line, diverging from it when forced to do so by a small copse. At the lip of Stebbing Brook, turn right downstream.

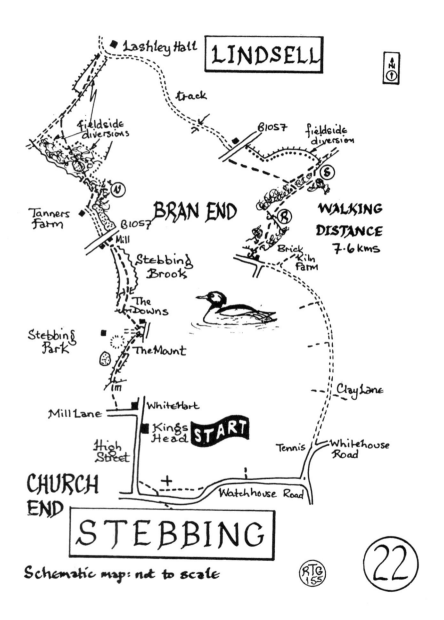

Lashley Hall

LINDSELL

track

B1057

fieldside
diversions

fieldside
diversion

Tanners
Farm

BRAN END

WALKING
DISTANCE
7.6 kms

B1057

Mill

Stebbing
Brook

Brick
Kiln
Farm

The
Downs

Stebbing
Park

The Mount

Clay Lane

Mill Lane

White Hart

Kings
Head   START

Tennis   Whitehouse
Road

High
Street

CHURCH
END

Watchhouse Road

STEBBING

Schematic map: not to scale

22

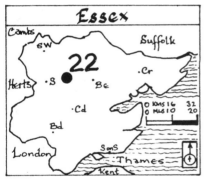

The Kings Head
High Street
Stebbing
Essex.

☎ 0371
856289

Day	Snacks		Meals	
	Ln	Eg	Ln	Eg
Sn	✓	✓		
M	✓			
T	✓	✓		
W	✓	✓		
Th	✓	✓		
F	✓	✓		
St	✓	✓		

Walk Profile

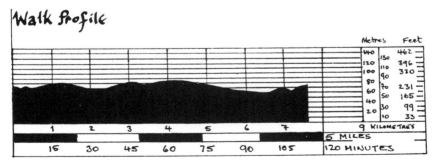

Waterfowl

Opt for the footbridge straight ahead S over the lesser waterway (**U.652255**) and walk the field-edge path with brookside trees on the left-hand side. Approach the waterfowls' delight at Tanners Farm, and share the drive out to Bran End's B1057 road.

Cross to find the continuation path behind the mill. It follows the right-hand hedge of the valley floor meadow, with the brook on the left-hand side. Six minutes from the mill diverge from the hedge to cross the brook by a bridge successfully constructed from a cylinder. Beyond it is a gated bridge in a high hedge and from the gate climb SE up the Downs to the cottages by the gate to Stebbing Park.

Castle

Cross the drive to the matching stile inside the road gateway, and descend the Downs S to overlook the flower-strewn mound in the castle moat. With a stile, a footbridge and a right-hand fence to steer by, the kissing gate to Stebbing cricket field is soon found.

Skirt the square to find an exit by a red brick wall on to Mill Lane. Turn left uphill and the smart appearance of The Kings Head is across High Street to the right. Remove or cover outdoor boots before going indoors please.

Pub Yarns

The 14th century church is distinguished by its stone screen. It once belonged to the Knights Hospitalers of St John. The tithe of £154 in 1755 was raised to £235 by 1785 and the clergy found gathering the increased taxes quite a battle.

The weather-boarded mill at the bottom of Mill Lane was grinding corn until 1960.

The Quaker Meeting House dates from the early 1700s.

The castle was built by Ranulf Peverel who also planted a vineyard in 1086.

The Park Farmhouse is Elizabethan.

Walk 23: Rayne's Welsh Princess

Pods Brook separates Rayne from Braintree, and along that boundary it becomes the river Brain, a tributary of the Blackwater below Witham. Through the attractive vale of Pods Brook is a network of popular paths, upon which this walk is composed.

Rayne's centre is clustered on the higher land favoured by the builders of ancient Stane Street. Now the A120 bypasses Rayne and the old Roman road has traffic ramps to discourage its use as a thoroughfare and to encourage a safer pedestrian environment. Holding a proud mid-position in the community is the Welsh Princess.

How to get there

Leave the M11 by Junction 8 and select the eastward A120 beyond Dunmow to Blakes End roundabout, where the Braintree bypass diverges from the Roman Stane Street. Stay with the older route where sleeping policemen bounce suspension systems as far as the Welsh Princess on the left-hand side, map reference 167TL728226.

What is there?

Rayne is a village clustered along Stane Street and the adjacent former railway. It is in the heart of Essex farmland and is near to a market at Braintree. There are Tudor farmhouses around and Rayne Foundry. Good community facilities include the church, the hall, the school, The Flitch Way and the pubs.

The Welsh Princess is a freehouse selling Adnams and Greene King ales and offering lunch time snacks and meals.

Walk details

Walking distance	9 kms (5.6 miles) needing about 135 minutes to stroll
Ordnance Survey maps	Landranger 167 Chelmsford & Harlow
	Pathfinder 1075 Great Dunmow & Braintree
Paths used	Rayne 10, 28, 8, 3, 4, 21
	Panfield 12, 11, 23, 4
	Great Saling 7, 4
District Council	Braintree

The Walk

Walk eastwards along The Street sidewalk to The Swan and turn on to Shalford Road as far as the war memorial. Join path 10 here to approach All Saints church and find the exit gate in the boundary wall. Turn left behind Rayne Hall and strike off right by the marker post on a mid-arable path heading for the vehicular bridge over Pods Brook (**V.733233**).

PANFIELD

Hall Road

GREAT SALING

⊗

Mounts

diversion to edge

diversion to edge

headland

headland

Perry Childs Farm

Midfield path

Ⓦ

headland

Park Farm

Ⓨ

Golden Grove

re-instated midfield paths

midfield path

footbridge

Ⓥ

midfield path

RAYNE

Pound Farm

Moors Farm

Pods Lane

START

Welsh Princess

Swan

The Street

Village Hall

WALKING DISTANCE
9 kms

Schematic Map: not to scale

RTG 156

㉓

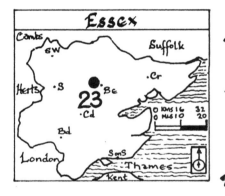

The Welsh
Princess
21 The Street
Rayne
CM7 8RW

☎ 0376
345 822

Day	Snacks		Meals	
	Ln	Eg	Ln	Eg
Sn	✓			
M	✓			
T	✓			
W	✓			
Th	✓			
F	✓			
St	✓			

Walk Profile

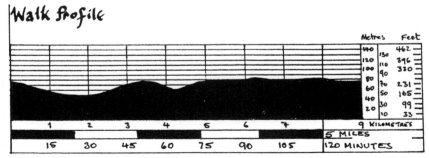

Pant Crossing

Cross the road but not the bridge to use path 8, fine tuned to be a brookside path, until the Sewerage Treatment Plant on the opposite bank is passed.

Beyond the compound the second trailer chassis serves as a bridge to carry the path to the Panfield side of the brook. Stay brookside as far as the next footbridge and climb out of the valley on a cultivation lane heading for the hedge bend of the western boundary. Join a headland and approach Panfield as far as a footbridge east of Perry Childs Farm **(W.730248)**.

Head for the seat on Hall Road and join the road by the double waymarks. Face oncoming traffic along the lane north-westwards as far as the signpost pointing right. The required westward path may be without its signpost, but it has vehicular width as it proceeds back in to a wooded part of Pods Brook valley. Fencing protects newly planted trees from mammals' nibbles.

Cradle Bridge

Move west of this compound with caution as springs saturate patches of ground. Descend to the footbridge in a meander bend **(X.718252)**. The ditch and path line on the far bank also act as a locating line to find the bridge.

Climb that line by the cypress hedge which deflects the path's exit slightly away from Mounts Farm. Adjust along Shalford Road to the signpost opposite the Farm and join the bridleway by the cottage garden greenhouse. Keep to the path hedge-side around the first bend and then a headland is joined at the next.

Golden Grove

Approach Park Farm and turn left as the headland enters an avenue of pine trees. Join the headland beyond the pond and swap sides of the boundary at the corner of Golden Grove **(Y.712243)**.

Clearly reinstated paths continue over a bi-concrete track to a stand of trees around a pond. Go left when over the footbridge and from the hedge end re-join Shalford Road along another clearly reinstated path.

Face oncoming traffic beyond Pound Farm and fork right on to Pods Lane by the Moors Farm entrance.

Flitchway

Cross Dunmow Road and enter Gatewood's drive to connect with The Flitchway. Turn left between twin footpath signposts to walk the old railway track. At the platform site of the former Rayne Station go left again and walk Station Road to re-join The Street not far from The Welsh Princess.

Pub landlords and bus drivers alike appreciate not having muddy footwear in areas of their concern. A pair of plastic shopping bags make lightweight and effective boot coverings.

Pub Yarns

The Flitch Way is a linear space open to the public, stretching 17 miles from Bishops Stortford to Braintree. It is both a good nature reserve and a pleasant walkway.

All Saints church dates from about 1510 and was rebuilt in 1841 with a tiered pinnacle above the tower's external turret.

Harvard University in the U S A has connections with John Bridge who set sail for America in 1632 and founded the College which became the University.

Is the Welsh Princess connected with any of the Royal Highnesses of similar title?

Walk 24: Layer De La Haye's Fox Tavern

Walking the lowland watersheds of eastern England is the sort of thing some fell walkers think other walkers do only in desperation. The land around Layer de la Haye is not even an obvious watershed, yet somewhere the drainage spills between the Roman River and Layer Brook swollen by Abberton's dam.

This is a truly lowland watershed walk. The quality of the walking experience is in the range of textures underfoot, the kaleidoscope of its changing horizons, and the zoom of focus from the longer views to the closer interest and back again. Walking like this, they say, is good for the soul as well as the heart!

How to get there

Slip left from the four-lane carriageway of the A12 at Lexden, signed (A134) and use the A604 E to join the A134 in Colchester, going S up the dual carriageway of Balkerne Hill, under the footbridge, to the roundabout with the police station on the S side. Use the B1022 Maldon Road exit and then take any one of the third, fourth or fifth residential roads uphill left to link with the B1026 on its two-way length. Turn right, pass the soccer floodlights, dip to cross the Roman River at Kingsford and climb to The Fox Tavern at Layer crossroads, map reference 168TL968200.

Buses	Osbornes services 1 & 10 from Colchester town
Trains	Colchester Town with above bus connections

What is there?

This village with a Norman name, is separated from Colchester by the wooded Roman River valley. The church is set away from the crossroads but most other village features; school, hall, recreation ground, shop, decorative sign etc. are found near the crossing known as Layer Fox in acknowledgement of the Tavern's dominating presence there.

The pub is friendly and serves food proudly along with ales such as Ruddles and Websters. Car parking is for patrons and cars should not be left there without the landlord's permission. Alternative car-parks are by the school, hall or church when they are not in use.

Walk details

Walking distance	8 kms (5 miles) requiring about 120 minutes to complete
Ordnance Survey maps	Landranger 168 Colchester & The Blackwater
	Pathfinders 1077 Colchester. 1099 Witham & Tiptree
Paths used	Layer de la Haye 4, 1, 3,14,15,16, 7.
District Council	Colchester

The Walk

From the Fox Tavern crossroads move over to the school in High Road and turn left on to New Cut and pass the Queen Elizabeth Hall. Ignore both the right bend and the left turn on to Bolls Lane, and press ahead on the gravel drive signed '99 down lane'. Two stiled gates signal the path by Woodland Cottage and a yellow arrow points left at a fork in the ensuing thorn tunnel.

Sylvan Setting

A quick glimpse of arable land is seen left before the path is swallowed under a canopy of branches at the concave corner of woodland. Internal fencing steers the path NNE to converge with another path using Oliver's footbridge over the Roman river in the Roman River Valley Nature Reserve (**Z.967210**).

Stay south of the river to return on the other path up the short steep slope and bearing left through a zone of younger growth before entering the top area of larger trees. A new fence on an old earth bank steers the path through the under culture of holly, dipping right to a plank bridge over a stream. Rise with the gravel path swinging left through another stiled gate to pass a pump and Friendly Cottage, both on the left-hand side, before crossing the B1026 to the stile beside Les Bois.

The Folly

Garden and field fencing steers the path through to The Folly. Go left by Somerville and right on to the silver birch lined gravel drive to The Kiln. As the drive swings left, a stile on the right-hand side offers an additional path option to get east of Black Barn.

Follow the fence down the grassy slope to the stile and proceed eastwards on a superb undulating path through mixed textures of small woods and smaller paddocks and grazing plots, where stiles are essential both to enable fence crossings and as navigational aids. Join the stony drive of Layer Mill just above the mill buildings. Go right uphill and right along Abberton Road until by Rockrose.

Bird Sanctuary

The opposite path, when unblinkered by the garden boundary of Pippins, offers great views across Abberton Reservoir, famous nationally as a bird-watching place. Hook right at the hedge end and join Field Farm

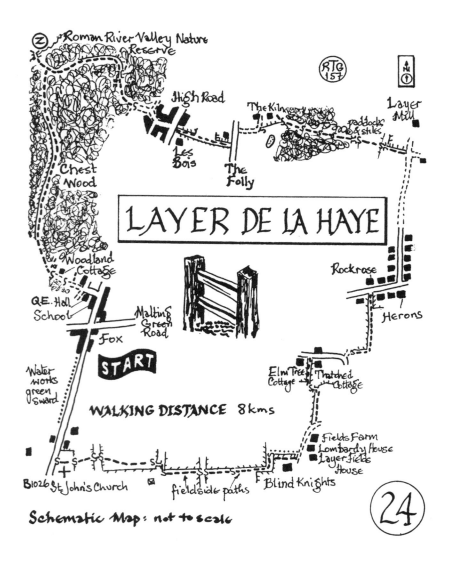

LAYER DE LA HAYE

WALKING DISTANCE 8kms

Schematic Map: not to scale

24

THE FOX TAVERN

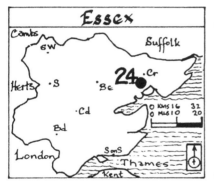

Essex

Combs
SW
Suffolk
24 .Cr
Herts .S .Be
.Cd
Bd
London SonS
.Thames
Kent

O KMS 16 32
O MLS 10 20

The Fox Tavern

Malting Green Road

Layer de la Haye

CO2 OJH

☎ 0206
   734351

Day	Snacks		Meals	
	Lh	E	Lh	E
Sn	✓	✓	✓	✓
M	✓	✓	✓	✓
T	✓	✓	✓	✓
W	✓	✓	✓	✓
Th	✓	✓	✓	✓
F	✓	✓	✓	✓
St	✓	✓	✓	✓

Walk Profile

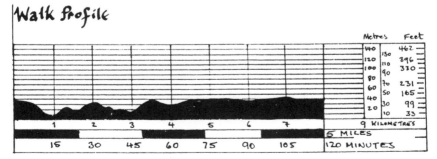

	Metres	Feet
	140 130	462
	120 110	396
	100 90	330
	80 70	231
	60 50	165
	40 30	99
	20 10	33

1 2 3 4 5 6 7 9 KILOMETRES

5 MILES

15 30 45 60 75 90 105 120 MINUTES

Road going uphill as far as another southward path opening. This one, between Thatched Cottage and Elm Tree Cottage, has new path furniture down to the bridge and up by the right-hand hedge to merge with an unmade section of Field Farm Road.

Blind Knights

Pursue it to the terminus at Blind Knights where the path has been pushed north side of the northern boundary to squeeze by the western edge of the tennis court and to behold closer views of the reservoir. Follow the right-hand hedging W over the stile to a double stiled crossing of Rye Lane and on to the stile close to a pylon.

Waterworks

Swap sides of the fence here via the footbridge and second stile. Continue W over the double stiled Wick Lane and then by mid field path towards the church. A stile allows entry to St John the Baptist's churchyard and another stile makes an exit on to the B1026 road.

Face the traffic flow right as far as Wick Farm, and then a broad greensward by the waterworks permits more pleasant progress to the 40 speed signs. Again face the oncoming traffic for a few more paces to the crossroads and The Fox Tavern. Change to less muddy shoes before entering the premises.

Pub Yarns

Has anyone suggested to you that Layer de la Haye is linked with the French river Loire, or with Leicestershire? Included, among the many explanations of the origins of this attractive name for this village, are theories that Layer stems from Legra. This is the base name for the other two far away places mentioned. The De La Haye is Norman and probably comes from Val de la Haye near Rouen.

One of the bells in St John the Baptist's church was cast in 1459 by Widow Sturdy in memory of her husband, a bell-founder of Sudbury.

Blind Knights is an arousing name. It dates from at least the twelfth century and was probably a hospital for wounded Crusaders well enough to travel home from the battlefields.

Walk 25: Kelvedon's Angel

The river Blackwater flows through Kelvedon, and once provided power for at least a couple of watermills to contribute to the settlement as found today. Like most other Essex rivers the Blackwater is generally eastward flowing, until it bends westward in Kelvedon to skirt the gravel-capped lump of London clay known as Braxted ridge and so shares an estuary with the river Chelmer. A pleasant walk ensues from The Angel at St Mary's Square to the watershed on the ridge and back down by other paths to the Blackwater valley.

How to get there

The A12 trunk road by-passes Kelvedon, and the spinal road through the settlement is the B1024 which fronts The Angel at the junction with Maldon Road, map reference 168TL860183.

Buses	Colchester - Chelmsford route 53
Trains	London Liverpool Street - Clacton on Sea line

What is there?

Kelvedon is an ancient settlement, probably the Roman Canonium, attractive to people though the ages for being at a crossing of the Blackwater on the London - Colchester route. Much parking in the busy main street effectively slows the traffic flow, thus reducing the noise if not the exhaust fumes. The street's frontages have not been developed in the modern everywhere-should-look-alike pattern and an attractive assortment of architectural enterprises remain on view. The Angel is a large accommodating Inn with both garden and restaurant. Snacks and meals are available as well as Ind Coope beers and a range of drinks. The car-park seems to enlarge St Mary's Square. Alternative parking may be found along Maldon Road's verges by the higher bridge.

Walk details

Walking distance	9 kms (5.7 miles). Allow 135 minutes to stroll
Ordnance Survey maps	Landranger sheet 168 Colchester & The Blackwater
	Pathfinder sheet 1099 Witham & Tiptree
Paths used	Kelvedon 26, 25, 15 in Braintree district
	Great Braxted 20 in Maldon district
	Tiptree 5, 4. Inworth 17, 16 in Colchester district

The Walk

Leave St Mary's Square by Maldon Road's sidewalk passing the library housed on a 1836 Aylett's School site. Cross the riverbridge by Gray's Mill and fork right to walk beside the river and then climb over the A12 road bridge. Fork left this time and when at field level, double back a

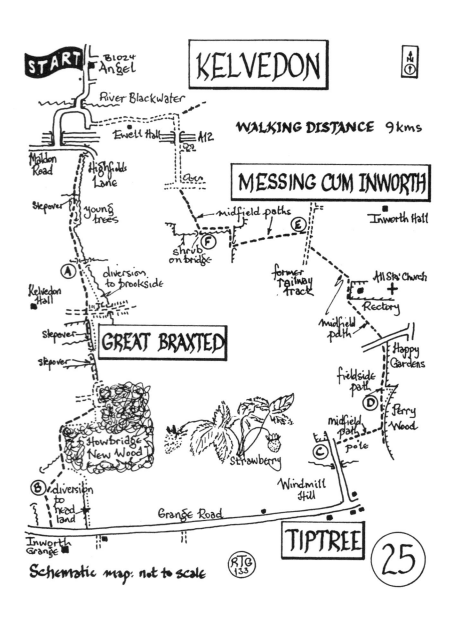

START · B1024 Angel

River Blackwater

KELVEDON

Ewell Hall · A12

Maldon Road

Highfields Lane

stepover · young trees

WALKING DISTANCE 9kms

MESSING CUM INWORTH

Inworth Hall

midfield paths

(F) shrub on bridge

(E)

(A) diversion to brookside

Kelvedon Hall

former railway track

All Sts' Church

Rectory

midfield path

GREAT BRAXTED

stepover

stepover

Happy Gardens

fieldside path

(D) Perry Wood

midfield path

Howbridge New Wood

Strawberry

midfield path · pole

(C)

Windmill Hill

(B) diversion to headland

Grange Road

Inworth Grange

TIPTREE

(25)

Schematic map: not to scale RTG 133

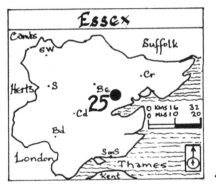

The Angel

St Mary's Square

Kelvedon

CO5 9B

0376
570445

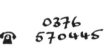

Day	Snacks		Meals	
	L/A	E/s	L/A	E/s
Sn	✓	✓	✓	✓
M	✓	✓	✓	✓
T	✓		✓	
W	✓	✓	✓	✓
Th	✓	✓	✓	✓
F	✓	✓	✓	✓
St	✓	✓	✓	✓

Walk Profile

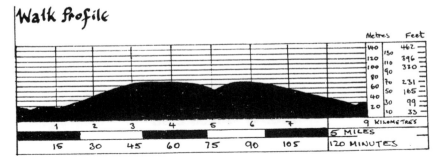

few paces to get alongside Jubb's brook flowing down from the ridge.

With the hedge and brook on the left-hand side, use the field-edge paths to the parish boundary bridge where Kelvedon path 26 becomes Great Braxted path 20 **(A.867168)**.

Brookside

In the next field diverge slightly from the brookside to meet the convex field-corner on the causeway track to Kelvedon Hall. Cross the track to continue southward alongside the hedge. The mapped route has an unbridged ditch, and its worn diversion goes east of the hedge until a cartbridge allows a reversion to the intended side.

Watershed

Pass around the western edge of Howbridge New Wood where the gradient demands more puff. From the SW corner strike off SE across the open field to the watershed where the stream beginning on the right flows in the catchment of the river Colne **(B.874159)**. Change direction to ESE and follow the invisible district boundary for a furlong out to Grange Road at a point midway along the tall foliage bounding Inworth Grange.

Windmill Hill

Face eastwards, and any oncoming traffic, along Grange Road from which good views, especially northwards to Lanham Green and Chalkney Woods, may be seen. Turn left again by Hill Wood to dip and climb Windmill Hill as far as the pumping station fence **(C.880170)**.

Use Tiptree path 5 to pass the mid-field pole and join path 4 midway along the western edge of Perry Wood. Resume hedge-side walking going northwards **(D. 882172)** to cross Inworth's lane by Happy Gardens and continue on path 17 mid-field towards the yew tree in the corner of the rectory garden.

Crab & Winkle Line

Stay outside the garden fence and from the next corner head WNW for the foliage growing from a shallow embankment of the former Tollesbury Light Railway. Walk the cindery track as far a gap and ramp in the left-hand hedge **(E.876180)**.

Now on path 16, cross the field SW towards a solitary oak tree and so locate the bridge in the field boundary. Over the bridge turn right beside the ditch and bridge in to the next field to go left alongside the connecting ditch as far as the bridge sprouting shrubbery **(F. 873178)**.

Dual Carriageway

On the last mid-field reinstated path of this walk head NW for the junction of tracks on Kelvedon path 25 and continue on the track NW to bridge over the A12 dual carriageway. Bend left with the track which becomes Ewell Hall Chase, passing a few picturesque dwellings en route to the bridge over the river Blackwater by Gray's Mill. With cleaned boots return to the Angel via Maldon Road.

Pub Yarns

Kelvedon is the Saxon Cynelaf's Hill settlement from whence Eaelric fought at the Battle of Hastings 1066.

St Mary the Virgin's church was restored in 1877, and All Saints church at Inworth was also restored in 1877 including the red brick tower.

Lord Western, Whig M P for the area, extended Felix Hall in 1830.

Charles Haddon Spurgeon was born in Kelvedon in 1834.

The Kelvedon to Tollesbury Light Railway was built to aid the marketing of farming and fishing products.

Walk 26: High Roding's Black Lion

The seven Rodings or Roothings - White, Margaret, Leaden, High, Berners, Aythorpe and Abbess plus their neighbours are in the catchment area of two rivers, the Can and the Roding.

It would seem that the river through Canfield is the Can, and the one starting with this walk south-eastwards of High Roding is the Roding. Not so. The young river that joins this walk out of High and Aythorpe Roding is the Can.

The Can flows on beyond the Walk to join the Wid at Writtle and is then central to the lovely riverside park landscapes in Chelmsford before contributing to the Chelmer.

How to get there

Leave the M 11 at junction 8 for the A120 eastwards to Dunmow. Use the A131 SE for 0.5 mile and turn acutely right on to B 184 towards Dunmow for 0.3 mile. Turn left on B184 which swings SSW for High Roding. The Black Lion is at the further end of the settlement on the right-hand side of the road, map reference 167TL602171.

Buses	346 Thursdays only; Great Dunmow - High Roding - Leaden Roding. Lodge's 33 Tuesdays, Fridays and Saturdays routed Good Easter - High Easter - Chelmsford
Trains	Chelmsford station and bus, bicycle or taxi to High Easter.

What is there?

High Roding is a long ribbon of a village sawn asunder by the B184 traffic on its axis. Like so many Essex villages, 13th century All Saints church is found away from the main settlement, and in this case it is west of the Black Lion overlooking the Roding valley.

The timbered pub has a restaurant, garden and a meeting room. Meals, snacks, Adnams and Ridleys ales are all included in the tariff.

Car parking is for patrons and vehicles should not be left there without the licensee's approval. Alternative parking may be found on verges by Yeumans Barn, Slough Bridge or High Easter's School Lane.

Walk details

Walking distance	9 kms (5.6 miles) needing about 135 minutes to stroll
Ordnance Survey maps	Landranger 167 Chelmsford & Harlow
	Pathfinder 1098 Great & Little Waltham
Paths used	High Roding 15, 16, 21, 22, 14, 12, 49.
	Aythorpe Roding 16, 18, 17, 22, 23, 32, 26, 33.
	High Easter 102, 101, 105, 21, 22, 2.
District Council	Uttlesford

The Walk

Turn left along the B184 from the Black Lion and cross to the panelled path northside of Cherise. Wind behind the gardens and out to the open field, turning right downhill at the path crossing by the hedge end. Turn left on the lane to Porters and climb to the waymarked path 21 right. Walk the field-edge with hedge on left-hand side. A pond in that hedge signals a divergence of the path from the hedge towards a stand of trees by the ditch running S to Yeumans.

Closer inspection reveals a double ditched junction at the parish boundary with Aythorpe Roding. Stay by the eastern ditch and swap to the eastern side of it when there is a convenient small tree to assist the crossing, for there is no bridge **(G.605161)**.

Yeumans

Walk by the side of the ditch out to the road by Yeumans Barn. Go left uphill and right on path 18 bending behind the residential barn, leaving the back hedge only to align with the mid-field overhead wires converging with a brookside path showing footfall marks.

Continue over the bridleway crossing SE between brook and paddock rails as far as the hedged confluence. Path 23 from beside the new reservoir crosses here. Veer right over the bridge and with the river Can on the left-hand side cross the next concrete bridge and swing left to cross the river on a matching bridge.

Tree Bridge

Go right, still downstream beside the river and when just beyond the game bird hatchery on the western side, switch back to that bank **(H.606144)**. The footbridge is sub-standard, the branches of a nearby tree being very necessary handholds. If in doubt, either return to the last bridge and traverse the western bank, or use the rescue bridge located a furlong WSW of Trotters.

Merrily the river ripples along between its vertically cut banks and the path follows it around the bend to face SE. Step over one small feeder ditch and merge with a headland down from Friar's Grange. Ninety seconds later a cradle-style footbridge should be in view **(J.611143)**.

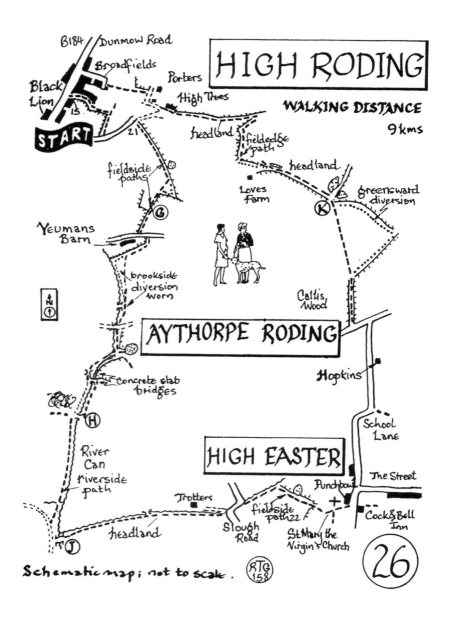

B184 / Dunmow Road

Broadfields

Black Lion

Porters

High Trees

START

15

21

HIGH RODING

WALKING DISTANCE

9 kms

headland

fieldedge path

headland

fieldside paths

Loves Farm

greensward diversion

Yeumans Barn

brookside diversion worn

Callis Wood

N

AYTHORPE RODING

concrete slab bridges

Hopkins

River Can riverside path

School Lane

The Street

HIGH EASTER

Trotters

fieldside path 22

Slough Road

St Mary the Virgin's Church

Punchbowl

Cock & Bell Inn

Schematic map; not to scale.

RTG 158

26

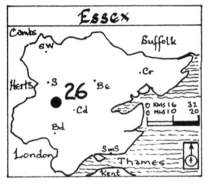

The Black Lion
High Roding
CM6 1NT

Day	Snacks		Meals	
	Ln	Eg	Ln	Eg
Sn	✓	✓		
M	✓	✓		
T	✓	✓		
W	✓	✓		
Th	✓	✓		
F	✓	✓		
St	✓	✓		

☎ 0371
872847

Walk Profile

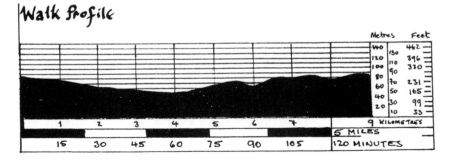

Head NE over the bridge and leave the valley with hedge on left-hand side to find High Easter's Slough Bridge.

High Easter

Stay south of the brook as far as the field corner and turn uphill by the hedge to the footbridged entry of St Mary the Virgin's churchyard. Join another path south of the mainly Norman church and exit E beside The Punchbowl and opposite The Cock & Bell Inn.

The next footpath of this parish was unwalkable, so the tarmac of School Lane NNW from The Punchbowl became relatively agreeable. Climb by Hopkins Farm and at the T-junction of the road go left for a few paces only before turning right on to a green lane which dips to a bridged entry of a large field bordered on two sides by trees.

Aythorpe

Now back in Aythorpe Roding, path 22 rises NW over the arable field, but there is an additional green verge around the right-hand edge to the same high exit by ponds at **K.613161**.

Use the headland W to Loves Farm, leaving the headland before it enters the steading to maintain the westerly direction as far as the next field corner. Turn right and walk the field edge path to a T-junction with another headland. Go left and approach the radio-masted lorry park by High Trees. Beware reversing vehicles and pass through to join a higher part of the lane used earlier.

Turn right, pass path junctions either side of the lane until just beyond Porters. When at the beginning of the byway, go left on footpath 12 across the field to the Broadfield's houses, joining the road by No 26 and going further west to pass the red mail box alongside Dunmow Road. Left is The Black Lion on the other side of the road. Change to an unmuddied pair of shoes before entering the pub please.

Pub Yarns

The Rodings (some say it rhymes with soothing) are Saxon settlements of the people of Hroth.

Overhead wires along the main road of High Roding were tidied up in 1967.

About the same time, a barn that was a YHA hostel became a splendid private residence.

Steam ploughing may have been witnessed in fields as early as 1863. Fowler's system of using two engines, one at either end of the field, proved popular as it could plough six furrows as fast a horse ploughed one. However, horses were more nimble at turning round at the end of the field.

Aythorpe Roding post windmill has been restored to working order and is open to the public on some summer Sundays.

High Easter's name could be derived from Eowestre which is a sheep fold.

St.Mary the Virgins church has an unusually wide chancel. Both pubs near the church have 15th century origins.

Sir John Gate of High Easter was Chancellor of the Duchy of Lancaster in 1552, but this office did not save him from being beheaded on Tower Hill in 1553 for his support for Lady Jane Grey.

Walk 27: Hempstead's Bluebell

Every drop of rain that falls on Essex is precious. A raindrop falling on Hempstead lands like a dice with a one in six chance of deciding with which river to flow. The Colne, Pant, Chelmer, Roding, Bourne and the Bumpstead Brook feeder to the Stour, all have nearby sources.

Hempstead is in the Pant catchment. The Pant changes its name to Blackwater at Bradford Street, Braintree and flows off toward the North Sea only to bend back at Coggeshall to join the Chelmer's estuary at Maldon. The big estuary was known as the Panta at Othona Camp in Roman times.

How to get there

From the A604's Little Chef at Birdbrook, turn on to the B1054 road through Steeple Bumpstead to Hempstead. The Bluebell is on the right-hand side just before the junction with the B1055 road, map reference 154TL633380.

Buses	A weekday service on the Haverhill to Saffron Walden route.
Trains	Audley End station (Wendens Ambo) West Anglia Line. Bus connection to Saffron Walden and another to Hempstead.

What is there?

Desirable cottages, many with ride-on mowers and stables are loosely clustered around the pub by the heart of Hempstead. The Bluebell, a bus shelter, and a memorial grace the High Street from which the village hall is set back. St Andrew the Apostle's church can be reached along Church Road beyond the pump and the Primitive Methodist chapel dated 1853.

The Bluebell is a popular village pub, where much may be heard about Dick Turpin the Highwayman. The large bar is augmented by a restaurant and a garden. There is car parking for patrons. Vehicles should not be left there whilst walking unless the landlord agrees to the arrangement. Alternative parking may be found on the Pollards Cross verge along Church Road.

Walk details

Walking distance	8 kms (5 miles) needing about 120 minutes to stroll
Ordnance Survey maps	Landranger 154 Cambridge & Newmarket
	Pathfinder 1051 Thaxted & Sible Hedingham
Paths used	Hempstead 42, 49, 46, 50, 26, 27, 1, 31, 32, 33, 31, 37.
	Great Sampford 2 plus some strides on Finchingfield 39
District Council	Uttlesford. The dozen extra strides being in Braintree.

The Walk

From the Bluebell cross High Street to climb the slope of Church Road and proceed beyond the speed de-restriction signs to the Church Farm Cottages with garden-paths bridged over the moat. On the right-hand side of the road a pair of garages guard the entrance to path 42 between them.

Cross the loose barbed wire carefully and follow the right-hand hedge to a narrowing of the downhill end of the field. Move SE over to the stile in the concave corner of the eastern hedge and use the mid-field path E to a plank bridge at a hedge-end-cum-path-junction.

The diagonal path is unclear across the arable crop and an additional path hugs the hedge down to a green lane.

Footbridge

Turn right to pass the waymark for the last path and locate the footbridge over the deep Pant-feeding brook left **(L.641374)**. Over the bridge let the left-hand hedge steer the path up, right, left and left again until opposite Fields Farm. To compensate for another unclear cross-field link, stay hedge-side until by the pond and cluster of trees where a headland is found crossing to the bungalow north of the farmstead. Veer right before the bungalow to unite with the right-of-way by a transformer on stilts, and make careful passage through the farmyard to the road.

Great Sampford Bridleway

Walk the country lane to round the southern side of Cabbages on a bridleway. The track leaves the shelter of hedges to use a mid-field line before dipping to be alongside the brook. Head NE out to the road by Lakehouse Farm, stepping in and out of Finchingfield parish in the process.

Turn left and approach Hempstead Wood. Join the bridleway along the southern edge of the trees. The bridleway follows the SW bend of the trees and three other paths leave the same corner **(M.656381)**.

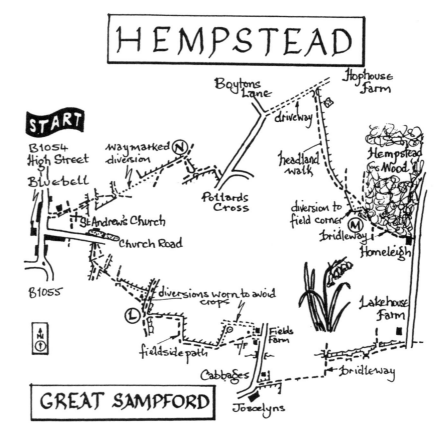

HEMPSTEAD

Hophouse Farm

Boytons Lane

driveway

START

B1054 High Street

waymarked diversion

N

Bluebell

headland walk

Hempstead Wood

St Andrew's Church

Pollards Cross

Church Road

diversion to field corner

M

bridleway

Homeleigh

B1055

diversions worn to avoid crops

L

Lakehouse Farm

fieldside path

Fields Farm

Cabbages

bridleway

GREAT SAMPFORD

Joscelyns

WALKING DISTANCE 8 kms

Schematic map: not to scale   RTG 159   27

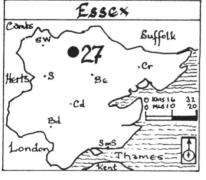

The Bluebell
Inn
High Street
Hempstead.
Essex.

☎ 0799
599486

Day	Snacks		Meals	
	Ln	Eg	Ln	Eg
Sn	✓		✓	
M	✓	✓	✓	✓
T	✓	✓	✓	✓
W	✓	✓	✓	✓
Th	✓	✓	✓	✓
F	✓	✓	✓	✓
St	✓	✓	✓	✓

 Walk Profile

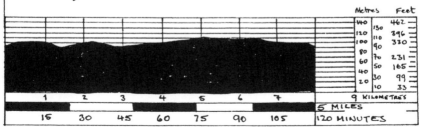

Pollards Cross

The middle one of these three is required. It starts SW alongside a left-hand hedge and bends right to a gap. Swap sides of the hedge in the gap to find a grassy headland around to the footbridge on to Hophouse drive. Walk the concrete drive WSW to Boytons Lane, continuing downhill to where path 31 completes the fourways of Pollards Cross.

Use this path and go round the hedgebend to find the plank bridge in to the next field. Go right with hedge on right-hand side, bending left to join path 33 from the corner gap **(N.640382)**.Stay by the hedge-side and follow the yellow arrows, rather than enter Church Farm and double out again.

The arrows point across the last neck of field towards an open sided barn. Stiles in paddock railings steer the path directly towards the church. Cross the lane to enter the churchyard and pass northside to find a field-edge path sloping down to the village hall and out to High Street almost opposite The Bluebell. Please change to indoor footwear before entering the pub for the sake of other customers' comfort.

Pub Yarns

Who was John Palmer in 1705? He changed his name to Richard Turpin and was executed at York Tyburn on 17th April 1739. The place where he was born has also changed its name from Bell to Bluebell.

The notoriety of a highwayman is such that his name lingers on in at least two other Walks in this book, and we are also still paying indirect royalties for our curiosity today.

He was preceded at Hempstead by a notable global personality. William Harvey 1578 - 1657 was Chief Physician to Charles I and was the discoverer of the circulation of blood. He is buried and commemorated in the parish church.

Walk 28: Greenstead Green's Hare & Hounds

The name Greenstead Green sounds good, and it is a charming settlement, as good, if not better than its name. Situated off the Essex trunk roads and overlooking the sylvan valley of Bourne Brook, it is a lovely base for a short exploration of the area towards the textile town of Halstead.

Many find it pleasant to hear the Essex accent hereabouts, it reminds them that East Saxon descendants have cousins many times removed in East Anglia speaking similarly in the Suffolk twang or Norfolk drawl.

How to get there

From the A604 east of Halstead, turn south on a country lane from the bottom of Bluebridge Hill near the buttresses of the old railway bridge which carried the Colne Valley Line. Climb with the lane to pass the tall spire of St James' church and merge with the road from Earls Colne before locating the Green by the crossroads. The Hare & Hounds is downside of the bus shelter nestled in the recreation ground's hedge, map reference 168TL822278.

Buses	Service 325 Wednesdays; Halstead to Braintree Service 329 Tuesdays, Fridays & Saturdays to Halstead. Halstead has daily services to Braintree and Colchester.
Trains	Braintree station and bus to Greenstead or Halstead

What is there?

The Green is a crossroads with a bus turn-around, cottages, pump, playing field, decorative sign plus one, sometimes two, pubs. The Hare & Hounds is a comfortable village pub serving real ale and bar snacks since refurbishment in the early nineties. A free house, it has a small car park for patrons only and cars should not be left there without the nod of the landlord. An alternative car-park is at the layby on top of Tidings Hill 812292.

Walk details

Distance	8 kms (5 miles) which takes about two hours to stroll
Ordnance Survey sheets	Landranger 168 Colchester & The Blackwater Pathfinder 1076 Coggeshall. With town streets on 1052
Paths used	Greenstead Green 23,22,24,28,30. Halstead 2.
District Council	Braintree

The Walk

With the front door of the Hare & Hounds behind, turn right, uphill and pass between the pump and the village sign to face oncoming traffic

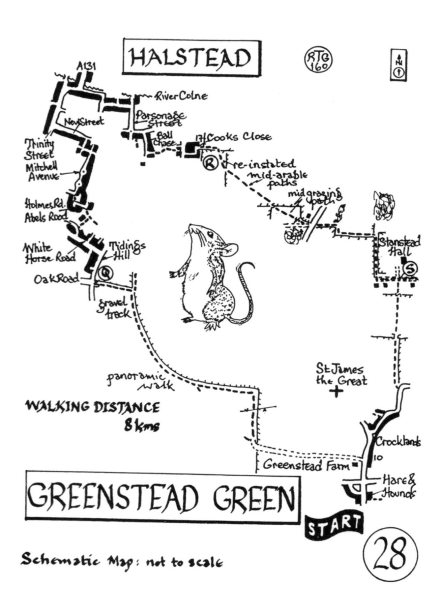

HALSTEAD

RTG 160

A131

River Colne

New Street

Parsonage Street

Ball Chase

17 Cooks Close

Trinity Street

Mitchell Avenue

re-instated mid-arable paths

mid grazing path

Holmes Rd.
Abels Road

Stanstead Hall

White Horse Road

Tidings Hill

Oak Road

gravel track

St James the Great

panoramic walk

Crocklands 10

WALKING DISTANCE
8 kms

Greenstead Farm

Hare & Hounds

GREENSTEAD GREEN

START

28

Schematic Map: not to scale

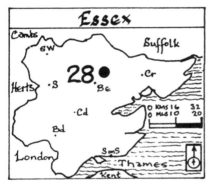

The Hare & Hounds

Grange Hill

Greenstead Green

CO9 1QZ

☎ 0787 477996

Day	Snacks		Meals	
	Ln	Eg	Ln	Eg
Sn	✓		✓	
M	✓	✓	✓	✓
T	✓	✓	✓	✓
W	✓	✓	✓	✓
Th	✓	✓	✓	✓
F	✓	✓	✓	✓
St	✓	✓	✓	✓

Walk Profile

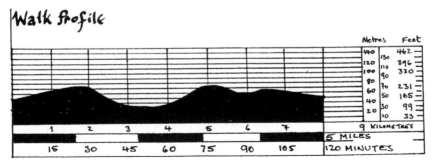

over the crossroads. A red mail box outside 10 Crocklands, is opposite Greenstead Farm's track.

Use this splendid track westwards, bending right when it enters the second large field. Pass under the wires and be steered by the hedge to divert away from the Pathfinder's hypotenuse line.

Enjoy the panoramic views across Bourne Brook valley to Plaistow Green and Gosfield, and stay with the same lane surface as it becomes path 22 and joins the Oak Road junction of Halstead **(Q.812292)**.

Halstead

Face the oncoming traffic of Tidings Hill right, and turn left on the sidewalk of White Horse Road. Use the second right turn, Abels Road, and veer right by the Co-op Store to the lock-up garages. Select a concrete path extending westwards to Holmes Road and continue to the beginning of Juniper Close where another concrete path leaves downhill right to the Ramsey Road - Mitchell Avenue junction.

Colne Valley

Use Mitchell Avenue and turn left on to narrow West Road, right on to Mount Pleasant, and left again on to New Street, to descend towards Halstead's bridges over the River Colne. Along New Street is a pleasure-garden and some of its paths make a short cut through to the A131 Trinity Street.

Turn right to enjoy more of Halstead, and when ready to leave go alongside the river Colne from the A131 bridge towards the Tourist Information Office. Go right, and quickly left on to Factory Lane and turn right by the Rescue station on Parsonage Street to find the mini-roundabout at the foot of Tidings Hill.

Lodge Cottage

Go left, ignore the path beside Teasels and turn right by the telephone box to climb Ball Chase cul de sac. Round the dwelling Linden Lee opposite Greenways and continue eastwards on footpath No.2 through a pending building site, and exit between the garden fences of Poplar Close left and 18 Stanstead Road right.

Cross to Cooks Close and find the downhill exit from the courtyard by No 17 to enter a field by an ash tree **(R.819298)**. Climb the headland, which is path 24 eastwards with hedge on right and at the gap, veer right on to a reinstated line through two sets of arable crops to the stile in a topside high hedge. Head diagonally across the pasture to Lodge Cottage and cross the road carefully to enter path 28.

Stanstead Hall

Dip to the wooded bridge and chicane right and left as dictated by the right-hand hedge and climb with the headland towards the southwest corner of Stanstead Wood.

Paddock rails are set far enough back from the hedge to allow passage southwards to Church Path Cottage. Go left on the drive shared with Oak Tree Cottage until by the turning to Stanstead Hall. Resume the southern journey, now on path 30, going from near the transformer on a pole **(S.827288)**, across the mown zone to the stepless stile, and then using the reinstated path through the arable crop to a bridge by a junction of hedges.

Continue southwards with high hedge on left-hand side, and the elegant spire of Greenstead Green church two fields over to the right, all the way to Crocklands Road.

Face the oncoming traffic until a sidewalk becomes available. Merge with the road from the church and return to first the post office and then the Green's crossroads. Please do not take muddy footwear in to the Hare & Hounds.

Pub Yarns

Stanstead Hall is part of a larger 16th century building.

The great weaving shed beside the river Colne was built in 1904. It was part of the Courtauld fabric industry. First silk was woven then crepe and finally rayon. The rattle of hundreds of looms continued until 1983.

The railway came to Halstead in 1860 and extended to Haverhill by 1863.

Among the new industries to arrive with the railway was Portways of tortoise stove fame. The passenger service closed in 1961 and goods traffic ceased in 1965.

Halstead's bigger school is named after Dame Mary Ramsey, founder of Halstead Grammar School in 1594.

Walk 29: Fryerning's Viper Inn

The daily round of everyday modern life keeps so many of us indoors that we need to give some priority to walking, just to get outdoors and notice the seasons passing by. A good place for a walk any season of the year is this area west of Chelmsford. Between Margaretting and Blackmore there are, under the canopy of trees, samples of Essex clays. Vigorous streams feeding the river Wid cut through typical thin layers of Essex heathland gravel to reveal these underlying clays. Wellies are recommended for this Walk if there has been recent rainfall.

How to get there

Leave the A12 trunk road at the B1002 Margaretting interchange, and turn off the NW slip road (approached either from the Chelmsford-bound carriageway or from the Wantz Road overbridge) on to Ivy Barns Lane by Furze Hill, signed "Highwood 3". Proceed along the pleasant lane to find The Viper Inn by the junction with Mill Green Road and Ingatestone Road, map reference 167TL641019.

Buses	None noticed
Trains	Ingatestone station and bicycle or taxi

What is there?

Mill Green is a green surrounded by woodlands, enough to make a forest. There is access to some of the woods via public paths that go under, rather than around, the canopy of broadleaves. Cottage roof corners poke through the foliage to announce their presence, and The Viper Inn is so situated, in a beautiful garden amid tall trees, a ready backdrop for the telling of adventure stories like Goldilocks or Little Red Riding Hood, or the other Hood - Robin.

The Viper is the only known pub with the name in the country. It is a freehouse serving Ruddles and other ales and has an attractive garden. Snacks are frequently available and there are facilities for disabled customers.

Walk details

Walking distance	8 kms (5 miles) requiring 120 minutes to stroll
Ordnance Survey maps	Landranger 167 Chelmsford & Harlow
	Pathfinder 1122 Chelmsford
Paths used	Fryerning's in Brentwood Borough district
	Highwood 29, 30, 26, 28, 12, 13 Margaretting's 2, 8. In Chelmsford Borough district

The Walk

Leave the front door of the Viper Inn and cross Mill Green Road with care to the opposite parking patch from which a tarmac drive disappears

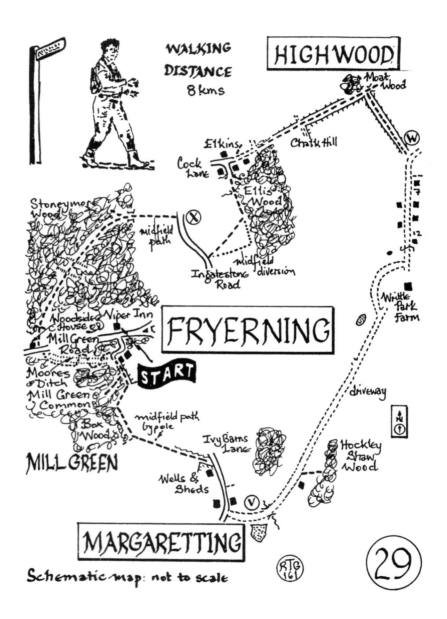

WALKING
DISTANCE
8 kms

HIGHWOOD

Moat Wood

Etkins

Cock Lane

Chalk Hill

W

Ellis Wood

Stoneymore Wood

midfield path

X

midfield diversion

Ingatestone Road

7

2

Woodside House

Viper Inn

Mill Green Road

FRYERNING

Writtle Park Farm

Moores Ditch

START

Mill Green Common

driveway

Box Wood

midfield path bypole

Ivy Barns Lane

N

MILL GREEN

Wells & Sheds

Hockley Shaw Wood

V

MARGARETTING

29

Schematic map: not to scale

RTG 161

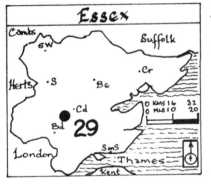

The Viper
Mill Green
CM4 0PS

☎ 0277
352010

Day	Snacks		Meals	
	Ln	Eg	Ln	Eg
Sn				
M	✓			
T	✓			
W	✓			
Th	✓			
F	✓			
St	✓			

Walk Profile

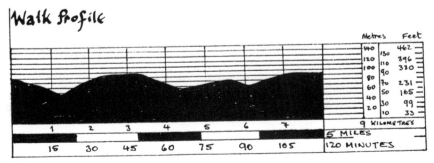

SE under the trees. Follow the drive over its sleeping policemen and around its double bend to leave the tarmac and crunch stones underfoot whilst passing west of Richard's Cottage.

A short passage between hedges leads to a fork of paths. Stay by the left-hand hedge and at the corner swap sides to walk the fieldside of the woodland boundary. The path bears left with the woodland edge and from the NE corner, takes a mid-field NE line by a pole, eventually sloping down to a ditch source and hedge. Keep this hedge on the left-hand side to cross a parish boundary and connect with Ivy Barns Lane by a garden corner bridge.

Wells & Sheds

Walk the greensward right to pass Wells & Sheds farm and cottages to the right-hand bend of the road. Fork left here opposite a transformer on stilts, to use an unmade road dipping to a brook bridge by a reservoir **(V.650025)**. Use the concrete road, or its greensward NNW between woodlands to bypass west side of Writtle Park Farmhouse and continue by the weather-vaned tower stump. As the road bends beyond cottage 7, turn left on to a green headland **(W.649040)** and approach the wooded site of old Moat Farm. Turn left again to head SW down Chalk Hill between fence left and hedged ditch right. At a lower level the fence is replaced by a woodland, Pools Lane joins in from the right and the surface becomes smoother as the dwellings of Cock Lane are reached.

Ellis Wood

Dip downhill left on a short road opposite Elkins, cross the bridge and climb the field-edge path beside Ellis Wood. Another bridge connects with the next field and a local diversion alongside the trees keeps the mid-field section to a minimum length.

Go right along Ingatestone Road and at the crest of the little hill turn left on to a mid-field track **(X.637024)** leading SW in to Stoneymore Wood. Bear left to a bridleway SSE through Deerslade Wood, across a system of banks and streams to re-enter Fryerning and emerge from the trees by Woodside House.

Moore's Ditch

Cross the road by the beware cattle sign and trace Moores Ditch ENE, serpentining across the earthworks several times under the trees to return to the tarmac drive not too far from Richard's Cottage. Turn left and trace the drive out to confront The Viper Inn again. Please remove muddy footwear before entering, or use the Tap Room as the notice suggests.

Pub Yarns

Where do some of the seeds for lovely colourful flowers like those in the Viper Inn garden come from? Many are produced in Essex in the warm area of light soils the other side of Chelmsford from Highwood. Fields coloured by primula, begonia, salvia, nemesia, lobelia, clarkia and many others, are in the business of seed-growing. Here purity is paramount and there has to be absolutely no risk of mixing. Bees are important pollinators, and more is done by brushes wielded by human hand.

A 17th century curate of Fryerning, is alleged to have declared to his bishop that the chief parochial problem was the people's proneness to adultery.

Much land around Mill Green Common belongs to Wadham College, Oxford. Sir Nicholas Wadham, founder of the College, acquired the manor from the Knights Hospitalers to whom it had been given by the family Mountfitchet. Wadham married a daughter of William Petre.

A medieval pottery thrived in the area, and later agricultural drain pipes were made from local clay.

Airey Neve MP, a minister for Northern Ireland in Mrs Thatcher's government murdered in the car-park of The Houses of Parliament, lived in Fryerning as a lad, and a memorial to him is in St Mary's church.

Highwood Parish, with St Paul's church, separated from Writtle in 1842.

Walk 30: Coggeshall's Fleece Inn

Essex clay is easy to tunnel and every good pub in the county has a tunnel story dating back to Reformation times and Coggeshall is not without its stories of tunnels. If old holes could be sold, Coggeshall would be the place to market them for it is a centre of commerce in antiquities. Some of the television Lovejoy antique sitcom scenes are shot in the village; but perhaps the best antique is PAYCOCKES a former wool merchant's dwelling managed by The National Trust, next door to The Fleece. Did their tunnels connect with the Old Abbey south of the river?

How to get there

Leave the A604 at Earls Colne to use the B1024 road S over the A120 junction and in to central Coggeshall. Turn right on to West Street by Robinsbrook bridge and find both PAYCOCKES and The Fleece on the left-hand side, map reference 168TL847224

Buses	Colchester - Stansted Airport service 133 by Eastern National
Trains	Nearest station Kelvedon connected by the Community Bus.

What is there?

Coggeshall is a large village with, in places, a small town atmosphere. It was a prosperous lace-making place. The Fleece Inn is an ancient public house with a garden extending towards the River Blackwater. Exterior walls have examples of Essex pargetting work.

Car parking for patrons is under the archway. Cars should not be left there without the permission of the landlord. Alternative parking is in Stock Street layby.

Walk details

Walking distance	8 kilometres (5 miles) requires about 120 minutes to stroll
	Ordnance Survey maps
	Landranger 168 Colchester & The Blackwater
	Pathfinder 1076 Coggeshall
Paths used	Coggeshall 18,11, 10, 33, 35, 37, Bradwell 47, 22.
District Council	Braintree

The Walk

Head for the village centre eastwards along the footway to Market End swinging left by the Clocktower to enter Stoneham Street. Pass the library housed in a former chapel and fork left at The Yorkshire Grey. Bridge Robinsbrook and continue up Ambridge Lane to a slight bend left.

A footpath signpost forks right **(A.845231)**. Use the reinstated path through the crop to the double stiled crossing of the A120. Move to be by the side of the ditch off the second stile, and a few paces northwards finds a bridge over a feeder ditch. The path continues along a reinstated line right of the woodland and left of Gatehouse Farm's moat **(B.841238)**.

Ha Ha

Turn left on the concrete drive and chicane right left at the lane junctions to approach Holfield Grange via an estate cottage. Where the track swings right towards the Grange, fork left over a stile and enter a pasture. The path swings right adjacent to the dovecote and diverges clearly from a ha-ha corner SSW out to the white stile by Hovell Road **(C.832231)**.

Descend the slope of the country lane to the busy Stane Street and turn right to pass the farmstead and cross the road to find Bradwell's Stock Street layby.

Ford

Approach Whiteshill Farm barn in the dip of the layby and turn left on to the old airfield concrete road under the pyloned cables. Watery Lane fords the River Blackwater and there is a sturdy footbridge adjacent upstream which allows a connection with Cuthedge Lane **(D.820221)**. To the right, a visit to Bradwell's Holy Trinity church is worth a short diversion.

Go uphill from the end of Watery Lane through the trees and turn left where Cuthedge Lane elbows right. Walk the headland in to the valley of the Blackwater and use the lower headland by a new reservoir and then the old West Mill to pass the gravel pit workings between foliage and fence.

Dick Nunn's Bridge

A waymarked crossing of the gravel road **(E.832221)** shows the path by the eastern extractive bank up to Curd Hall. Go left and right around the paddock railings to join the main track, going eastwards as far as the first hedge left. Turn back in to the valley alongside this hedgerow and cross the footbridge in to the zone of willow trees with the underculture

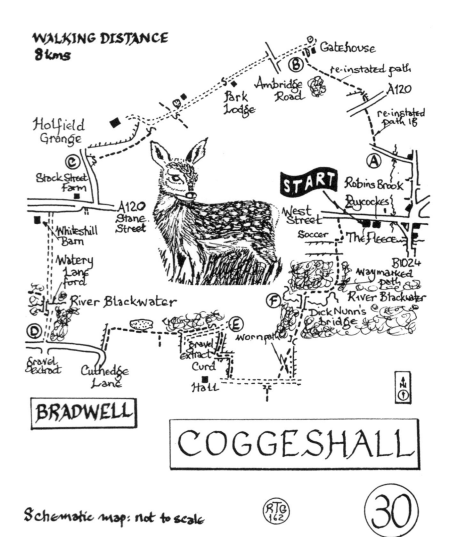

WALKING DISTANCE
8 kms

Gatehouse

Ⓑ
re-instated path

Ambridge
Road
A120

Park
Lodge

re-instated
path 1B

Holfield
Grange

Ⓐ

Ⓒ
Robins Brook

Stock Street
Farm
Daycockes

START

A120
Stane
Street

West
Street

Soccer
The Fleece

Whiteshill
Barn

B1024

Watery
Lane
ford

Waymarked
path

River Blackwater
River Blackwater

Ⓕ
Dick Nunn's
bridge

Ⓓ

Ⓔ
Wornpath

Gravel
extract

Cuthedge
Lane

Gravel
extract
Curd
Hall

BRADWELL

COGGESHALL

Schematic map: not to scale

Ⓡ Ⓣ Ⓖ
162

㉚

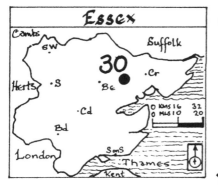

The Fleece Inn
27 West Street
Coggeshall
CO6 1NS

☎ 0376
561412

Day	Snacks		Meals	
	Lu	Eg	Lu	Eg
Sn				✓
M	✓			
T	✓			
W	✓	✓		
Th	✓	✓		
F	✓	✓		
St	✓	✓		

Walk Profile

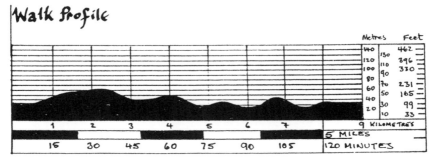

of comfrey.

Straddling a bend of the Blackwater is Dick Nunn's handsome bridge, 101 years old in 1993 **(F.837219)**. It is essential to this walk, and the ensuing waymarked path winds under the trees to a stile south of Coggeshall Town's touchline. Work a way around the stadium to West Street, going right to The National Trusts' gem at Paycockes by The Fleece. Please swap to a less muddy pair of shoes before entering the pub.

Pub Yarns

St.Nicholas Chapel in Coggeshall Hamlet was part of a Cistercian Abbey. Nearby, The Grange Barn was restored with much acclaim in 1986.

Gum for early postage stamps was made from acacia trees grown in Coggeshall. G.P. Swinborne & Co. Ltd. are experts at the clarification of beers and wines. They operate from the Isinglass factory in West Street.

John Kay, inventor of the flying shuttle, had looms in Coggeshall.

Coggeshall has a distinctive niche in the history of lace making. In 1851 the industry was at its peak. Straw plaiting also had a centre of operations in Coggeshall.

Great wool merchants used their wealth to endow East Anglia with magnificent churches and superior dwellings. Thomas Paycocke, a master clothier, helped Coggeshall to one of each. He moved to Coggeshall from Clare in 1450. He operated an outwork system much loathed in many places, but respected as fair when run by Paycocke.

How and why did Coggeshall become involved with the flower and vegetable seed trade?

Walk 31: Boreham's Cock Inn

The Chelmer & Blackwater Navigation is about two hundred years old, for it was started, if not completed in 1793. A basin in Chelmsford was linked to the river Chelmer which was canalised through to Beeleigh, where with adroit adjustment of levels, the canal passes to the course of the river Blackwater to Heybridge and then along a new cut to the estuary wall at Colliers' Reach.

Today there are many more recreational than commercial craft afloat on the canal, but we enjoy the legacy of the canal, kept clean as a reservoir, tree-lined to provide willow timber, available for sport - boating, canoeing, fishing and walking.

This Walk follows a track contouring the valley side, before sampling the towpath and diverting to a church of great charm.

How to get there

Boreham is on the B1137 and is bypassed by the A12. Join the B1137 from the A138 Springfield overhead roundabout off the A12. Select the eastward turning and traverse Main Road to locate the Cock Inn by the Waltham Road junction, map reference 167TL761105.

Buses	Services 53 Colchester - Chelmsford and 91/2 Maldon - Chelmsford
Trains	Nearest station is Hatfield Peverel connected by above buses

What is there?

Ribbon development along Main Road disguises a charming village centre best explored on foot. The Cock Inn commands the busy junction with Waltham Road by its bridge over the A12. The bar stocks Adnams and Ridleys and other ales to enhance a good snack and restaurant meal menu. A bus shelter huddles on the corner of the inn's extended car-park, and cars should not be left there without the say so of the landlord. Anglers have created alternative car parking by both the road bridges over the Chelmer.

Walk details

Walking distance	8.3 kms (5.2 miles) needing 125 minutes to stroll
Ordnance Survey maps	Landranger 167 Chelmsford & Harlow
	Pathfinder 1122 Chelmsford, and a few metres on 1098
Paths used	Hatfield Peverel 45 in Braintree district
	Little Baddow 3, 59, 5 and 1 plus Boreham's 39, 40, 37, 34, and 47 in Chelmsford Borough district.

The Walk

From The Cock Inn cross the road to the bus shelter and head southwards across the small field to a footbridge linking with the next very

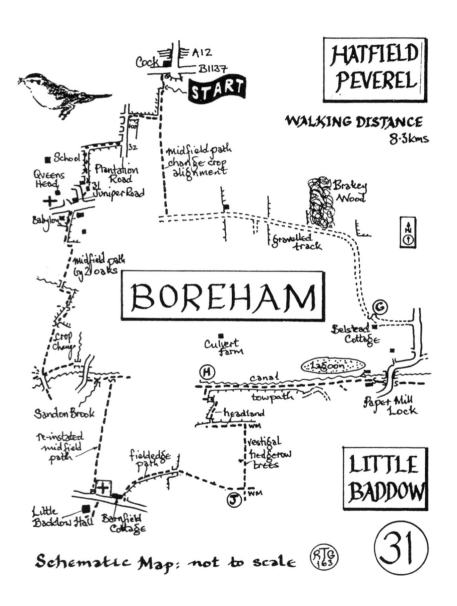

Cock

A12
B1137
START

HATFIELD PEVEREL

WALKING DISTANCE
8·3kms

School
Queens Head
Plantation Road
Juniper Road
31
32
Babylon

midfield path change crop alignment

Brakey Wood

gravelled track

midfield path by 2 oaks

BOREHAM

crop change

Culvert farm

Belstead Cottage

Lagoon

H

canal
towpath

Paper Mill Lock

Sandon Brook

re-instated midfield path

fieldedge path

headland

WM

vestigal hedgerow trees

LITTLE BADDOW

Little Baddow Hall

Barnfield Cottage

J

WM

(31)

Schematic Map: not to scale

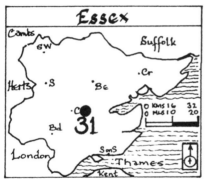

The Cock Inn

Main Road

Boreham

CM3 3AA

0245
467284

Day	Snacks		Meals	
	Ln	Eg	Ln	Eg
Sn	√	√	√	√
M	√	√	√	√
T	√	√	√	√
W	√	√	√	√
Th	√	√	√	√
F	√	√	√	√
St	√	√	√	√

Walk Profile

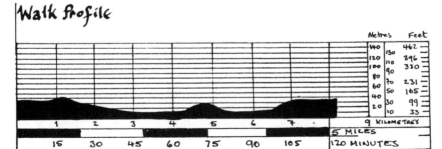

large field. Follow the right-hand hedge to its end by a path junction, and then use the grassy SSW mid-field path through to a gravelled lane. Turn left to chase this lane straight to, and just beyond, Brakey Wood where the lane bends to end at Belstead Cottage (**G.775093**).

Paper Mill Lock

Share the Cottage drive out to the road and turn downhill. There are no sidewalks. Cross the Chelmer at Paper Mill Lock and use the gate on the SW corner of the bridge for access to the towpath. Pass the Navigation Company Headquarters and follow the lip of the canal. The towpath merges with a headland for a short stretch. Watch out for the meander and veer right to regain the towpath as far as a waymarked footpath junction (**H.767085**) south of Culvert Farm.

Turn left off the towpath and left again over the cartbridge to go south over another bridge, almost hidden by reeds and rushes growing tall from the dykes, and gain access to an arable field.

Waymarks

The path is well waymarked. It goes left along the hedge-side for a minute and then takes the line of some trees in a vestigial hedgeline SSE to a crossing path waymark (**J.769082**). Turn right to face Little Baddow church still a couple of fields away. Footfalls have reinstated the path WSW to a footbridge in a hedgebend.

Little Baddow Hall

Cross the bridge follow the left-hand hedge out to Barnfield Cottage. Downhill right is St Mary the Virgin's church and opposite is the fifteenth century timber-framed Hall.

Steps surmount the bank at the SW corner of the churchyard and the ensuing path leaves the NE corner of this lovely setting to cross the arable acres on a perfectly reinstated path to a stile on the canal towpath.

Sandon Brook feeds the Chelmer nearby and a sturdy footbridge crosses the confluence. Cross the road and the river to join the north side towpath where a footbridge crosses another confluence. Ahead a footbridge rises high before Little Baddow Mill lock and four other paths meet the steps of its northern side.

Classic Alignment

Select the one heading NNE towards Boreham church to make a classic mill to church alignment. A change-crop line steers the path to a bridge and rises to the higher level of the next field. A stile midway along the left-hand hedge indicates both a cross-path and a swapping of the church-bound path to the western side of the hedge. Bear left to walk brookside as far as the cradle type footbridge.

The rising path passes two mid-field oak trees and chicanes left and right around a tennis court to be steered by Babylon boundary out to Boreham village centre. St Andrew's centrally towered church is over to the left beyond the useful cluster of mail box and bus stops. Over Church Road right is the Juniper Road junction with a footpath veering right of the telephone kiosk to pass bungalow 31.

Proceed along the eastern boundary of a schoolfield and turn right to join Plantation Road by dwelling 32. Turn left and look for the path beside dwelling 100. Enter here and follow the left-hand hedge through to the path junction used earlier. A final left turn faces The Cock, two fields and a road width away. Please swap to non-muddied footwear before entering the pub.

Pub Yarns

Thomas Radcliffe, Earl of Sussex, Viceroy in Ireland, built New Hall. Much can be read about him in St.Andrew's church. Boreham House noted for its reflective lake alongside the main road was built by Benjamin Hoare. Later, it was home to some of the Tyrells of Essex fame, and is now owned by Fords as an Essex base for their international action.

The lagoons by the canal are the residue of gravel extraction. About 80,000,000 cubic metres were mined each year and the green fields of Essex were being plundered twice. Once to get at the gold gravel, and secondly to be smothered in grey concrete. This Chelmer valley site saw early pitscaping projects as a result of public pressure.

Henry Mildmay has a monument in St Mary's church, Little Baddow.

This is a selection from our guides to walking and cycling in the great outdoors throughout England and Wales:

South-East

RAMBLES FROM NETWORK SOUTH EAST – Clive Higgs *(£6.95)*

LONDON BUS-TOP TOURIST – John Wittich *(£6.95)*

BEST PUB WALKS IN & AROUND LONDON – Ruth Herman *(£6.95)*

BY-WAY TRAVELS SOUTH OF LONDON – Geoff Marshall *(£6.95)*

TEA SHOP WALKS IN THE CHILTERNS – Jean Patefield *(£6.95)*

CYCLING IN THE CHILTERNS – Henry Tindell *(£7.95)*

PUB WALKS IN OXFORDSHIRE – Lawrence Main *(£6.95)*

CYCLING IN OXFORDSHIRE – Susan Dunne *(£6.95)*

Cycling . . .

CYCLE UK! The essential guide to leisure cycling – Les Lumsdon *(£9.95)*

OFF-BEAT CYCLING & MOUNTAIN BIKING IN THE PEAK DISTRICT – Clive Smith *(£6.95)*

MORE OFF-BEAT CYCLING IN THE PEAK DISTRICT – Clive Smith *(£6.95)*

50 BEST CYCLE RIDES IN CHESHIRE – edited by Graham Beech *(£7.95)*

CYCLING IN THE COTSWOLDS – Stephen Hill *(£6.95)*

CYCLING IN SOUTH WALES – Rosemary Evans *(£7.95)*

CYCLING IN LINCOLNSHIRE – Penny & Bill Howe *(£7.95)*

CYCLING IN NORTH STAFFORDSHIRE – Linda Wain *(£7.95)*

Country Walking . . .

FIFTY CLASSIC WALKS IN THE PENNINES – Terry Marsh *(£8.95)*

CHALLENGING WALKS IN NORTH-WEST BRITAIN – Ron Astley *(£9.95)*

RAMBLES IN NORTH WALES – Roger Redfern

HERITAGE WALKS IN THE PEAK DISTRICT – Clive Price